CALL OUT

LEARN TO LOVE YOURSELF AND FIND LOVE

SENADA CINDY NUREDIN

Published by Richter Publishing LLC www.richterpublishing.com

Book Cover Design: Richter Publishing stock images by Shutterstock

Editors: Haley Morton & Monica San Nicolas

Book Formatting: Monica San Nicolas

ISBN: 978-1-954094-05-5 Paperback

DISCLAIMER

This book is designed to provide information on relationships only. This information is provided and sold with the knowledge that the publisher and author do not offer any legal or medical advice. In the case of a need for any such expertise consult with the appropriate professional. This book does not contain all information available on the subject. This book has not been created to be specific to any individual people or organization's situation or needs. Reasonable efforts have been made to make this book as accurate as possible. However, there may be typographical and or content errors. Therefore, this book should serve only as a general guide. This book contains information that might be dated or erroneous and is intended only to educate and entertain. The author and publisher shall have no liability or responsibility to any person or entity regarding any loss or damage incurred, or alleged to have incurred, directly or indirectly, by the information contained in this book or as a result of anyone acting or failing to act upon the information in this book. You hereby agree never to sue and to hold the author and publisher harmless from any and all claims arising out of the information contained in this book. You hereby agree to be bound by this disclaimer, covenant not to sue and release. You may return this book within the guaranteed time period for a full refund. In the interest of full disclosure, this book may contain affiliate links that might pay the author or publisher a commission upon any purchase from the company. While the author and publisher take no responsibility for any virus or technical issues that could be caused by such links, the business practices of these companies and/or the performance of any product or service, the author or publisher have used the product or service and make a recommendation in good faith based on that experience. All characters appearing in this work have given permission. Any resemblance to other real persons, living or dead, is purely coincidental. The opinions and stories in this book are the views of the authors and not those of the publisher.

DEDICATION

To those who inspired it and will not read it.

CONTENTS

ACKNOWLEDGMENTS

I'd like to thank my loving and supportive husband
for always putting up with my shit.

INTRODUCTION

Are you learning to love yourself, or trying to find love? If you're reading this, chances are that you're in one of two worlds: one where you're looking for love or one where you think you've found it—I've been in both. Finding your one true love is not easy. When has a healthy relationship come easily? Never. We work hard, live harder, and at the end of the day we just want a loyal, compatible man by our side to share life's greatest moments with. A man who will love us, worship us, and treat us with the level of respect that we deserve. No matter what type of woman you are – girly, tomboy, divorced, single mom, whatever – you all have a million things to worry about every day. Now mix in the deadly dose of love, and *voila!* You've officially gone crazy.

I've devoted my entire life to understanding the male mind and how they interpret relationships, and I know what works and what doesn't. I can empathize with the pain of almost every woman. Whether it's a woman who's been scorned, a woman who's desperate for love, or even the woman who wants nothing to do with a man. There are women who spend too much time on a man who, in the end, doesn't give them the time of day. There are women who refuse to open themselves to a life of love. There are women who did open themselves, only to find that it would've been better if they hadn't. The combinations are endless, and our patience is running low.

I'm writing this book to help women find love. Whether that's finding love within yourself or finding a partner to share your life with, we all need that feeling of belonging, to feel safe and at home. You should feel as if you have life by the balls, and I want to give that feeling to you. I want to teach you that you can push past the barriers of your past heartbreaks, that true love is possible. There is someone out there for you, and it's my mission to help you find that person. I have found that within myself, and with my partner. Not everyone gets to say that they truly love themselves, or that they've found destined love. I've found both and it's the greatest feeling in the world.

This book is your new DIY tutorial on men. I have cracked the key that drives their minds. I have lived this book over and over again, day after day. What makes me qualified? I do not have a PhD in men. I do not have a Masters in dickology. What do I have? I have the balls to call out all the types of men in this world. Thanks to the metaphorical balls I carry between my legs, you can now hang a little to the left, or right, and enjoy the facts I've collected over the course of 20 years.

Within this book, you'll find yourself going through a whirlwind of helpful tips and tricks that will help you live your best life. You'll learn what it means to call someone out. You'll begin where we all find ourselves: usually in a broken cycle, and you'll make your way through the self-pity party. Once you're ready to put your big girl panties on, you're going to go on an adventure that will make you feel like Wonder Woman. You'll learn to listen to your sixth sense, and if you already do, you'll learn how to tap into your magical superpower. You'll understand that gut feeling we all have, and you'll learn that it's a gift from God herself. Once we've set the tone and you're in the right mental state, you'll be introduced to the different types of men and their corresponding personality types. A few men will come to mind once we get there, and hopefully it'll help you build up the courage to call out the men in your life: The Character, The Sweetheart, The Mistake, and The Bad Boy. And in Me, Myself and I, you'll learn the importance of loving yourself. And finally, we'll talk about The One and what to look for in your forever person. I'll sum it all up in The Point. And then we'll start to shift our focus to what else you need in your life in order to make a relationship with yourself and a partner work. The first thing is a good support system. And then you'll witness firsthand how therapy can save someone and a relationship. Life is hard, love is harder. Tell me something I don't know, right? You'll experience the difficulties of life and love within this book. It has some twists and turns so be sure to grab yourself a bottle of wine because you're in for a wild ride.

CALL OUT

Calling a man out is basically telling him when he does something shitty, telling it how it is, not bottling it up. When a relationship ends, do you tell the world what went wrong? Or do you keep it all in and let both of you make the same mistakes in your next relationship? We want to call him out because clearly these men can't hear us when we're leaving hints or being polite. We, as women, need to call out the men who treat us poorly. If not for ourselves, then for the next girl. We need to understand where we went wrong, and we need to put it out in the universe. Calling out a man isn't to disgrace the man, it's not to shun him, or hurt him, it's to make things better, to communicate our needs and how men aren't meeting them. It's a way for us women to understand why this man wasn't right for us and what we need to do different for when Mr. Right comes along.

I have encountered and interviewed dozens of women, all in different situations. Dating, divorced, married, heartbroken, you name it, I've sat down with them. One commonality between these women is that they're blinded by the idea of true love. They expect to find it with someone who usually turns out to be the wrong someone. You can't force true love, nor create it. It just happens. Divorcees started off happily ever after, and eventually the reality of the marriage came to light. They were incompatible. Husband and wife forcing each other's beliefs, concerns, and ways of life upon each other like the plague. Alcoholic husband and a stay-at-home mom, work wife and daddy-daycare father, an emotionally stable woman with a not so mentally stable husband. Every relationship is different, much like men. These women all stated that they had a sixth sense in regard to their significant other yet chose to go against it. They forced a relationship with their partner, hoping for the best, wishing the other would change, and that is not how you should enter or stay in a relationship. If something feels off, there is usually something bigger behind that. There is truth behind it, and the sadness behind all of this is that we know something is wrong, yet we choose to not believe it. Fight the urge to force yourself to be with someone because you love them. Don't let those faults and issues between you go unsaid. Tell them what is wrong. Call them out!

Calling out a man, pointing out his typical man flaws, may not seem like the kindest course of action in a relationship. However, it might be the difference between endless frustration with your partner and happily ever after. As women, we go through life trying to figure ourselves out and the paths we want to take. We learn from both our mistakes and our successes, whether it is while we're getting an education, building a career, or experiencing disastrous love. My strong, older sister Sabrina recently went through an ugly divorce with a narcissistic man. She loved him unconditionally and gave him everything. Literally everything. Time, support, love, kids, money, patience, you name it and she gave it to him. In the end, it wasn't enough. She was left heartbroken. Everything she did, every tactic she tried wasn't good enough for him. There were so many tears and endless nights where she would cry herself to sleep. Now, she's learned from the experience and she is the most Zen person you could meet. She lives life to the fullest and doesn't let any man distract her from life's priorities. The pieces that were once broken, have been put back together in the most beautiful way. We come across many obstacles during our journey and we overcome them, learning each time.

Some women are strong and can go through life with their heads up and tatas out, walking with confidence to their destination. You have to love a woman like that because no matter what obstacle she encounters, she dodges it. Even if she gets hit, she keeps on walking with a smile on her face. Even those women who are less confident with their walk, with their head slightly facing the ground, there's no shame in that. Eventually you will go through something that will give you the security you need to take on the world. Regardless of how you walk down your path, or which way you go when you face a fork in the road, there's that one ancient trap that gets the best of all of us: the sweet, enduring feeling of love. It can be as deadly as the dagger that killed Juliet in the Shakespearean tragedy.

Along this winding, slippery road of life, we pick up these men that, in the end, aren't anything but hitchhikers to keep the ride interesting. We find a man, pick him up, enjoy his company for a certain amount of time, then kick him to the curb. Either we automatically pick up another man or we keep driving down our chosen path until we see a man who catches our eye. Either way, the never-ending highway of love is an ocean-deep pool of emotions that keeps us on our toes. Not every man will be a Prince Charming, but we can learn something from each one and we have the opportunity to teach each one something, too.

As women, we can think of a million reasons to keep the faults of our past partners to ourselves. Maybe it's a lack of time, lack of interest or a somewhat nervous feeling of what others will think. Maybe you're worried the man won't take the constructive criticism well. And plus, whenever the relationship ends, it's difficult to express in detail what really went wrong. Having 'Call Out List' could help. When you feel in your gut, in that womanly-sixth-sense that something is wrong, write it down. Write down exactly what it was that made your gut turn, write down exactly what it was that you wish your partner would have done, and don't sugar coat it. It doesn't matter if you keep this list to yourself or you take it to your partner or to the world to work through, just having all your call-outs in one spot will change the way you view dating. It will help you get some perspective on your relationship too.

Most women, when they're done with a man, would rather not waste any more time on him. When they leave the relationship, they usually end it with anger, envy, confusion or maybe even happiness. When you're done with a man, you should be happy. Some women are happy because they got rid of the loser, dead weight. Other women are happy because they've lived through a new experience and are relishing their newfound freedom. And other women are happy simply because they ended things gracefully. You are probably in too much pain or anger to dwell on it any longer or you're at peace enough to just move on. But there's something to be said about putting it all out on the table, showing him what you: a person who knows him better than most, really think about him. I mean, you've already spent whatever amount of time on him so why not take that extra minute, hour, or day to at least make the end of that relationship worthwhile. Take that extra time for yourself, to figure out who that man really was.

Calling someone out is an idea that has always existed. A good way to start is to you call yourself out. This is a solid foundation for establishing new behavior or changing an old one. Let's say you're out on a first date and you order a salad. You notice that throughout the date that your partner is losing interest as the conversation goes on. You can't help but wonder what's going wrong. Fast forward to when you get home alone, and you notice that there's a piece of salad stuck in your teeth. You can't help but laugh at yourself. You'll probably call your friends and laugh it off, making funny comments about yourself and the situation you just survived. If you are able to laugh at something stupid that you did, and you recognize exactly what it was about that situation that made it so funny, you better yourself. You know not to do whatever it was again, because you will end up looking foolish. The same idea applies to call a man out. You call him out because the guy has done something to you that he should never do to a woman again. You call him out because you want him to learn, the way you learn from your own mistakes. You call him out to plant a seed in his brain that he isn't perfect and can make mistakes. Not every man is the same, so don't walk around screaming your head off about how every guy is exactly the same and why can't there be one different for you. There are plenty of men who carry different personalities; you just need to stop going after the crazies, and naming their faults can help you avoid those types of men in the future.

Every individual has a call out list and might not even know it. How about the guy you and your girlfriends joke about and gave a funny nickname for whatever it is he did? Well, that's a form of a call out. You're calling him out by putting his actions out there in the world, even if it's just between you and your entourage. No matter what circumstance your relationship ended on, it's a good feeling to have a call out list. My list consists of many breeds. The man who stalked me, the one I stalked, the one whose breath stunk, and the one who turned out to be my cousin. You naturally feel better.

Learn to laugh at yourself, and even others if the situation calls for it. They say laughter is good for the soul and is actually a form of healing. Loving yourself is hard enough, dating is even harder. Don't take life so seriously and understand that if you can call yourself out, you're already half way there!

SHOOT HIGH, AIM LOW

Recently, a coworker of mine was expressing her emotions regarding her love life. She has a "perfect man" list that covers everything that would make up her dream man. I will tell you now that, realistically, getting a man with all those things is not going to happen. However, having high expectations at least raises the bar for who you finally settle down with. You don't want to have low expectations because then you will eventually settle for something even lower than that. No one is perfect. That's why each of us must come up with a 'perfect partner list' with some ideals and some non-negotiables on it.

This list can have any number of things on it. One item from my list is being able to deal with the other person's baggage. I have always said that a happy, successful marriage is not how much you love the other person, but how much of them you can tolerate. If your future husband can put up with all the baggage you come with, the maintenance you require, attention you want or need, without complaining or looking elsewhere, then he's The One. If you can handle all your future husband's issues, ticks, bad habits, whatever it is, if you can put up with all of that and not go crazy, then he is The One.

For my coworker, finding someone who could relate to her background was on her list. She is foreign, and she said the first time around she married an American man. She was in love with him, he loved her, they wanted to get married and start a family. Now that they have been divorced for a handful of years, she has met a man that is close to meeting her perfect man list, and she told me he's from the same country she is. Meeting this new man, she found it much easier to connect with someone who came from a similar background to her. They just understand her on a rare level. This foundation is already sturdy, and they can build a future together. It makes understanding each other easier, the connection between them stronger, and the bond longer lasting. For them, a similar background was on their Perfect Partner list. I'm not saying that The One for you is strictly within your religion, ethnicity, or zip code; but you should think about what might be on your Perfect Man list and start looking for people who fit those qualities.

SUMMARY

No matter what is on your list, whether it's blue eyes and brown hair or a big 401k, make sure you keep your standards high and hold yourself to those non-negotiables. Otherwise, you will end up not learning from your past mistakes and continue to be in relationships that just don't work. I'm going to challenge you to write that list. Be honest with yourself and recognize your needs, no need to be realistic at this stage. Who is your Prince Charming? Put him on paper so you have standards to hold yourself to.

THE CYCLE AND THE SHIT CAKE

Getting stuck in a cycle in a relationship is natural. Going round and round, feeling the same way day after day, talking until you're blue in the face – these are symptoms that indicate that you might be stuck in a cycle. I know this cycle all too well. My husband and I have been together for nine years, and we still find ourselves stuck in them, as do other married couples I know. The key to avoiding this deadly trap is knowing when to jump out of the car before it explodes. Dramatic, I know, but so are relationships. When you or your significant other are feeling stuck, one of you must be the bigger man. You must step back, say, "Okay, this clearly isn't working," and make that grand gesture so you can break the cycle. You can't get yourself all worked up, stuck in a fog, you must break the spell and hope your partner is willing to work with you. Nothing will get fixed if both people aren't trying. It starts with one person speaking up, suggesting that you do something else. After being in couples' counseling and nearly giving up on our relationship, our counselor put it in terms we could understand:

> *A relationship is like a recipe. Imagine your favorite cake, and you know the ingredients you need for that cake to come out perfect. You follow the recipe, and your cake comes out delicious. The next time you want cake, you stray*

from the recipe, and add too much of this or not enough of that. Your cake tastes like shit: sweet, but full of it. The same goes for relationships. You have to find a good recipe.

My husband and I took this advice to heart. Our cake requires one coffee date a day, a minimum of three hugs a day, at least a dozen kisses, and about an hour or more of uninterrupted quiet time where I get to read, or watch TV, and he plays his video games. Listen to your love languages, listen to your partner, and listen to the status of your relationship. Only you and your partner know if your relationship is successful. The status of your relationship is determined by where you're at romantically. If you're stuck in a cycle, your relationship recipe is not good. Your cake is shit. Ditch the recipe you've been using and start over.

You don't have to have the same mother tongue to communicate. If your better half has a specific love language, you must speak that language. Even if it's only a few words, that's better than nothing. Because then they'll understand you. If you speak a few words of their language, and they speak a few words of yours, well then, you've generated a great foundation for a successful relationship recipe. Write that shit down. Put it on the fridge if you have to. If your partner needs a hug a day, make sure your recipe has one hug a day in it. If you need to hear that you're loved or valued, make sure your relationship recipe says that. You can tweak and add to your recipe at any time to fit your needs, but you don't want to eat a shit cake. So, don't make one.

After a while, you'll master your relationship, ingredient by ingredient, to the point that you've perfected the recipe. Then it'll just be a habit, a good habit, with great rewards, not like gambling or getting addicted to drugs. And congratulations, you've just broken the cycle. It's a great feeling, welcome aboard!

SUMMARY

Just because you broke the cycle, doesn't mean it'll stay broken. Shit always needs fixing. Relationships always need attention. Communication is key. If you're unable to communicate with your significant other, you're screwed. That usually means one of you is focusing your energy elsewhere, and let's not turn into a Lifetime movie. If you struggle with the communication factor in your relationship, then think back to when you started becoming one. Did you ever communicate? Were you ever able to sit together as one and work out your concerns or excitements with words? Words are important and listening to them even more so. You don't just talk to talk; you talk so someone will listen. Think about that the next time your significant other is trying to open up. I know I tend to block out my husband when he tells me about his day. I don't feel bad and I'm not the only one. His work interests are not my interests. But because I love him, I'll retain every other word and I'm able to communicate back to him. Let your special someone know that you hear them, that you care, that you are listening by taking note of the things they need every day. Those ingredients will create the best damn cake you ever made. Only then will your open communication result in positive action.

SINGLE SELF-PITY PARTY

If you're single and looking for love, good for you! Enjoy it! Life is short and settling down with the wrong person is not worth it. There is so much life and love to live, it's not worth forcing something just to say you've settled down. By traveling the world, or your hometown if you're broke, and experiencing new things, you're broadening your mating pool, expanding your mind to new and endless opportunities. The old saying is true, you must first love yourself before you can love someone else. If you're with someone just because they love you, but you don't love yourself, there's no guarantee that will last because as humans, we're constantly evolving and growing. Self-love, self-care, and being selfish are necessary for any human being. You can't forget about you. Whether you're single or not, taking care of yourself is number one. You don't like your job? Find a new one. You don't like your hair? Change it. Your body? YMCA offers financial assistance memberships if you need it (trust me on that, I know. I need it.) Another way to change your body is to listen to it. Eat healthier, go for yearly checkups, take a walk, do whatever you need to for your body to feel good.

The energy you give to the world is the energy you will get back. If you're having a bad day and everyone around you is being a dick, take a look in the mirror because not every person out there is a dick. You might in fact be the dick. And that's okay! But you have to stop pitying yourself and start reflecting. If every single female out there would appreciate the freedom she has, the world would be an even more dangerous place. Don't be the woman who takes it for granted. I don't regret most decisions I've made, and I've made some bad ones. But the one thing I wish I could do is go back to when I was single and follow the advice I'm giving you now. There were so many opportunities I didn't feel I deserved. So many men I didn't think I was good enough for, and so many ideas I had that I didn't have the confidence to pull through with. My sob story doesn't have to be yours. If you ask any married woman if there was something different she would have done when she was single, the ones who aren't lying will tell you the same thing: Take advantage while you have it, don't stress about finding love, and just love yourself. Being single means you don't always have to care about what people think about you or what they say about you. That goes for my single parents too! The right man will come around. Love yourself, find confidence within yourself, try new things, go to new places, and something great will happen.

As we evolve and grow, so do our taste buds and the things we desire. I might think I'm in love with Bob, but after seeing a new country, or living a new experience, I'll say screw Bob. This happens all too often, so my advice is to live a little. Try new things, travel, eat new foods, read a book you normally wouldn't, see a movie that's outside of your genre. Just do something different. Different is the key word. If you're looking for love, and you're stuck in this single self-pity party, do something you normally wouldn't.

For me, it was going on a spontaneous Canada work trip because I was the only one with a passport. That trip cost me a boring ass relationship, one that was new, and the guy was in jail. A goddamn pen pal. It cost me a jailbird pen pal and gained me a man who is now my husband. I'm not the type of person to willingly leave my comfort zone, not without some liquid courage, but in this instance, I was stuck in a single self-pity party, and at my lowest. Clearly, if I thought I could find love from a jailbird pen pal. So, I went to Canada, of all places, and found love. I reconnected with my now husband during a layover in New York City. I was on my way back home, and when he found out that I would be in his neck of the woods, we just had to meet up. He met me at the hotel where I was staying, and I decided that instead of sharing a bed with a friend, I'd share a bed with the man who had me mesmerized. That one night changed my life forever. The point is, put yourself out there. Not too literally (diseases are raging out there) but safely and responsibly put yourself out there.

Being single is beautiful. You don't have to answer to anyone, you don't have to worry about anyone other than yourself really. When I was single, I took my freedom for granted. I didn't appreciate the calmness of life, the endless opportunities. I always felt stuck, rushed, and ready to find love. Even if you're the type of person who needs someone to love you (there's no shame in that), you should take a step back and appreciate the value of your single, ready to mingle lifestyle. If you want to feel loved, there are ways of finding that without jeopardizing your mental state or time. Find a friend with benefits, or just a friend. Enjoy being able to innocently flirt with a cute guy at the grocery store or going on a first date. Most women hate starting over, having to reconnect with someone, learning all the basics all over again. But there is a beauty in first dates. The first and most exciting factor to first dates is they could potentially be the last of all your first dates. You get to see that there are all different kinds of men out there.

The most terrifying part of first dates is that it's possibly the first time you're meeting this person. You may not know anything about them besides their name. Luckily for single women, nowadays there's a thing called Google. Do your due diligence, ladies. Do not go out with someone until you've Googled them. Make sure there are no mugshots or horror stories from a crazy ex on a blog somewhere. Don't just view the photos on their social media, check out the tagged photos. We all know we look like different people when we're tagged in a photo versus the photos we choose to filter and post. Dating has become an Olympic sport with today's technology. You can know a man's entire family history, educational background, likes, dislikes, before you even meet. Don't be afraid of taking out some of the mystery behind a man, there's always the chance that there's some scary fact about a person you'd rather find out before you meet them instead of 20 years into the marriage.

But even if you've done your Googling, you can never be too careful. Make sure you have yourself a battle buddy. Have a good friend with you on first dates. No, not sitting at the same table as you, but order her a bottle of wine and an appetizer. Let your best bitch live a little at the bar while she stalks your date from afar. It's always better to have someone there making sure you're safe, and if the date ends up being a bust, you now have a tipsy bad bitch ready to talk shit about your date. Don't forget about that bottle of wine. It helps. If things happen to go well on your date, make sure you're sharing your phone's location with your friend, that way she has a way to keep track of you when you're doing the walk of shame in the morning. Give her the thumbs up, and have yourself a fun, protected time.

SUMMARY

Look in the mirror and be the bad bitch that you are. We all have something to bring into this world. Sitting around doing nothing isn't going to find you love, nor will it make you love yourself. Feeling sorry for yourself isn't an option. If it were, I'd still be stuck in a single self-pity party, and not married to the man of my dreams with two beautiful children. Take on the world one day at a time.

WOMEN WARRIORS

Women are warriors, and you have to remember that in a relationship. Your power can either be dulled or fed by a man. You have to learn how to spot the ones who will support you and the ones who will drag you down.

Life as a woman is hard enough without the concept of finding love interfering. We are strong, fierce, beautiful creatures. We are able to create life itself, but we're so often given the short end of the stick. We're hard on ourselves, as is everyone else. We struggle between work and family life, a balance that is impossible to keep up with. Yet we stand tall, taking whatever life throws at us. We are able to overcome any obstacle life flings our way, but we also can get stuck in a rut and struggle to get ourselves out. But when we do get out of the rut, there's no stopping us. The point of this topic is to remind my fellow women warriors that we will fall down. Life will knock us down. It's okay. It's acceptable, and it's normal. You're not the only strong woman who feels weak sometimes.

If you're in a relationship and you doubt your womanhood. It is not up to the man to make you feel powerful and almighty. Granted, you need a man who's going to feed the fire in your life; however, you create your own fire. You think a caveman created fire? More like a cavewoman. The caveman just collected the wood to keep the fire going. Much like the cave people, we can close ourselves off in a dark, wet environment. A woman with a strong, supportive man by her side can make magic happen.

A woman with no man on her side can also make magic. Don't get it twisted. It's not the man that gets a woman to shine, but the woman herself. The amount of blood we lose each month would terrify a man, but for a woman, that gives us the opportunity to create life. Coincidence? I think not. Women are far stronger than men in the sense that mentally and physically, we can multi-task to the point where we seem to have eight arms and eyes on the back of our heads with 20/20 vision. Use your womanhood to your advantage. Never let a man control you and remember that being a woman warrior is a gift from a higher power.

Women warriors come in all forms, shapes and colors. Married, single, dating, engaged, single mothers, adoptive mothers, working mothers, big boned, Victoria's Secret skinny, red hair, blonde hair, brown hair, it doesn't matter. We all share the power of being a woman. We have a sixth sense that allows us to feel things others can't. Some of us can sense the goodness in a person, some know when someone's about to enter a room. Whatever your superpower, use it. To find love, to keep love, to love yourself.

There are some women out there who use their powers to break down other women. To the women who are homewreckers and cheaters, you do not classify as a woman warrior. Why? Because there is a sacred bond between women, much like the bro code, there is an unspoken rule. Women should not shame other women, we should not steal from one another, nor destroy another woman's household. There are plenty of men in the world, no one needs to take one who's spoken for. It's uncalled for. For the homewreckers reading this, you're not on the HGTV network, so you're not DIYing someone else's marriage. If, for whatever reason, you come across a married man, and the two of you have some type of connection, sexual or not, and you both want to pursue it. Pick up the phone, drive to the house, or send a god damn text to the woman warrior you are about to disrespect. Do not ruin what another woman has built, do not feel entitled to steal another woman's hard work, her love, or life.

In high school, I had a tendency to home-wreck. I learned my lesson young to leave another girl's man alone. Being married, almost married, or in a serious relationship where you share assets, children, or even a god damn burrito, there's too much to lose to justify cheating. You can never find love in a man who is already spoken for. Chances are that man will never leave his wife and if he magically does, the way you get a man is the way you lose a man. If you cheat with a man who is spoken for, and you end up with him, bet your ass he'll lose you the same way he found you. They are thinking with their other head. The mini one. I don't care how big he says it is. You will destroy yourself and the other woman.

SUMMARY

Support your fellow woman warrior. Life is hard enough without another woman beating you down. Men do that to us enough, we don't have to do it to each other. If you see another woman struggling or feeling down, reach out. They could turn out to be your new best friend. Be that person. Women who grow together, often drink wine together. Who doesn't love wine? Or if you're like me, drink vodka. Less calories, more fun.

THE SIXTH SENSE

Are you with the wrong man? If I just created a spark within you, listen to your sixth sense. We have instincts that tug at our gut every day. Little voices in the back of our minds that speak up when he forgets our anniversary or calls us 'woman' instead of our names. That feeling, that voice that's telling you to get out, is your sixth sense. If a man gives you a bad feeling at the beginning, he'll still be giving you one in 10 months. That sixth sense is there to protect you, so let it.

If you don't feel excitement at least once a day when looking at him, you have to think about what purpose he really has in your life. When you first meet a man, you just know. I don't care what people say. Don't let the aftershock, that blurred vision we all get after we meet or date a man for the first time, blur your sixth sense. We see what we want to see, versus what's really in front of us. Every man I've ever met I got a vibe from. Without exception. Every time I ignore the feeling, I end up learning it was a mistake the hard way. The cheater I gave too many chances to, the selfish asshole that I made excuses for, the high school sweetheart that I knew would end up a criminal who I wasted years on who did, in fact, turn out to be a criminal. Many women have a tendency to want to nurture others, and that's fine for having kids or if you're a caregiver or medical provider but your husband shouldn't be as much work as a child. You're not raising him; you're supposed to be in a partnership.

The sixth sense in a woman is a power that men don't often understand. My husband will get mad at me, often saying that I'm a crazy bitch, because I'll be standoffish to people the second I meet them. Well buddy, here's a reality check: I'm listening to my sixth sense. Mama didn't raise a fool. I know when a woman is coming onto my man, I know when a salesperson is trying to scam me, and I know when I can get away with a good bargain. I listen to that feeling in the pit of my stomach. It rises within me in certain situations and over the years, after making many mistakes, I learned to listen, to feel for the familiar sense that will guide me in the right direction.

My mom is the master of the sixth sense, like Mr. Miagi from *The Karate Kid*. When I was a kid, that bitch always knew when I was up to no good. Her words still haunt me, and I now I haunt my own children with them. "I know everything. The things you think you got away with are only because I let you." That is the definition of a sixth sense, ladies. That inner power works not only on potential lovers, but with friends, kids, and even a random person on the street. You just know.

There are men who will respect your sixth sense and there are men who don't understand women at all. A good man will look the other way on purpose when another good-looking woman enters the restaurant or runs down the sidewalk in nothing but dental floss. I still get annoyed with my husband. That's a part of marriage. He didn't finish his latest construction project in our house, he hasn't cooked dinner in a month, he spends way too much time on his fish tank. Within those moments of "I want to kill him", I smile because I can't believe how good I've got it. He understands the way I operate. He has the manual in his back pocket. Find you a man that will keep your manual on hand for any situation. Never feel alone, abandoned or disrespected again.

As kids, we've all asked the question, how do you know when you've found The One? "You just know," they would say. What do you mean we just know? The real answer should be: your sixth sense will tell you. I've dated many men. There is always, and I mean always, a feeling I get with my sixth sense. You just know whether he's a creep, or a keeper. For my single-ready-to-mingle readers, brush up on your sixth sense cause that little inner bitch won't steer you wrong.

If you're a woman and you don't feel like you have a sixth sense, there's good news and bad news. I always like to hear bad news first, so here it is. You have some work ahead of you. You have to learn to love yourself. Start by learning your body, what makes you happy and even what makes you sad. You can't learn to listen to your sixth sense if you don't know how to listen to your body. Women are born with sixth senses, but not every woman knows how to listen to it. Stress, priorities and life can get the best of us, but the good news is: you have it! We're born with an infused sixth sense that only we can understand. Like your favorite drink, it's made up of different ingredients, as are you. You need to know what you're made of before you can master your taste. Once you do, indulge in your tastiness because it will lead to amazing things.

SUMMARY

In short, you want to be able to tune into your sixth sense. You need to listen to your body and your intuition. We all have that power, some of us are just more in sync than others. Use this as an exercise: when you meet someone, what's the first feeling you get before you even speak to them? Now, after you've spoken to them, how do you feel? Your feeling of this person might change, or it might not. But by doing this small exercise, you'll learn to listen to your mind and body. Don't act out of impulse, but instead, through your own energy.

DON'T CRY FOR ME ARGENTINA

Or as I tend to tell my five-year-old son, do not cry for those who don't cry for you. Don't waste your precious energy on those types of people. If they want to be a part of your life, they will make it happen. Don't force it. Romantic relationships are the hardest connection to make and keep in life. You don't want to force it because it's like trying to plug an iPhone charger into an Android. Something's going to break and, in life, it'll end up being your heart.

You need to find someone compatible for you. Someone who can understand your emotions without you having to explain yourself every step of the way. Yes, communication is key. But another idea to keep in mind is that you should be able to be in the same room with your significant other and share the silence. Silence is equally important as communication. Like the white space on a canvas, the silence acts as an enhancement for the beauty that is the canvas – or in this case, your relationship.

If you feel you're not ready to be in a relationship because you're suffering from a broken heart, don't be in one. There are billions of people in this world, many of whom are suffering from heartbreak. Women seem to feel the need to write novels to the man who broke their heart. Some men know what they did, they know how they hurt you. You don't need to go and let them know how much they hurt you. And then you have the oblivious men, the men who are so wrapped up in their own world they have no idea what they did. That type of man doesn't know he hurt you, or how he hurt you, and in those cases by all means reach out and let him know how you feel. But for those men who know what they did, who hurt you and broke your heart, confronting them for closure won't help you heal. Don't confuse this advice with some of the things I mentioned about calling men out. By all means, call those selfish men out, but don't contact him hoping that he'll make you feel better about your break up. The difference between calling a man out and confronting a man, is that you put your emotional needs to the side when calling them out. When you confront a man it's about moving forward. It's about the two of you. For example, if a man led you on for months and then ghosted you when it came time to get serious – you might want to let him know how much he hurt you, confront him about how much time he wasted, and overall how shitty of a thing that was to do. Whereas, if you're going to call him out, you'll want to be able to laugh at the fact that this man ghosted you. It's about what he does in the future, not so much about the relationship you had with him. Both calling a man out and confronting a man are necessary, and learning the art of when to do one or the other is a skill that will save you a lot of heartache.

Now, if you feel like you want to contact a man you know you shouldn't, call or text your best friend instead. Don't have a best friend? Then dial a random ass number, because it's better to be venting to a complete stranger than to vent to the man who hurt you. Both the man who hurt you and the stranger will care equally about what you have to say – and they won't care much. The man who broke your heart did you a favor. He saved you years of heartache and headaches.

Much like car insurance, men are easily replaceable, and you can collect different quotes from multiple resources to know if the man is worth putting your time in to. This chapter is about not crying for those who don't cry for you. So now that we know what to do with an ex, how do we know the man we want to start a relationship is worth it? As I've mentioned, technology is our friend. Use Google to your advantage. Google his name to make sure there are no outstanding warrants, use the search engine to find his social media accounts, make sure there aren't any X-rated websites that he's associated with. I personally recommend checking the area sex offender registry, like www.meganslaw.com and/or county arrest records if you feel the need. If you find a man you might be interested in but aren't sure, feel free to stalk his life. Don't invest in an online dating site. Use the technology you already have to find a potential dating mate. The luxury of this is that you not only save money, but you have a project to focus on so you start to forget the last guy. You also can see this man's life in real time. His hobbies, interests, career path, friends and family. Now, if you're reading this, I don't want to hear your story on the I.D. channel. Don't use this friendly information to kidnap anyone but use it to find love.

Men will find it weird if you stalk them online, especially if you're requesting them, their family, friends, sending emails or liking and commenting on every post or picture. Do not do that. I repeat. Do not engage. If you happen to come across a man who you're interested in whose life seems to intertwine with yours, or you just find him extremely good-looking, check to see if he checks in to a specific location. "Bump" into him. Make your own romantic comedy come to life. But if this isn't an option, just send a friend request and take it from there. Tell him Cindy sent you.

SUMMARY

We've all had our fair share of dating disasters, so I'm sure you all know what I mean when I say you don't want to date someone who doesn't care about you in the way you need. There are a lot of men out there and it may seem overwhelming to try to find someone to date, but the internet is there to help you and so am I. If you have an ex you want to reach out to, remember this chapter, remember your sixth sense and remember that some men just can't give you the closure you need, you have to find it within yourself.

GOD IS A WOMAN

Are you always the type of woman who takes care of herself? Have you ever had a man take care of you? No, not physically. I mean emotionally, financially, and okay yes, physically. To the women who are constantly taking care of others with no one to take care of her, I applaud you – but, you're doing it wrong. Take time for yourself but find a significant other who can help build you up instead of tearing you down.

Don't be the girl who tries too hard to get a guy or to keep him. Those girls usually don't get too far in life and for those of them who do, they're probably unhappy. I used to be the girl who tried too hard to keep a man. The only thing that did was drive him away. He'd run far and fast – in the opposite direction.

When I fall, I fall hard. I love the fairytales we heard as little girls, or the movies we watched and wished happened to us. I tried to reenact all those romantic scenarios to fit my own love life and it always ended badly. Like very bad. But the guy in each scenario made it off pretty good, while I was always left hurt and a little less 'me'. Never forget who you are as a woman. It's easy to forget who you truly are when we, as women, are constantly facing the pressure of other people's opinions. Whether it be the way we look, the way we act, our professions, how we are in the kitchen or even how we perform in bed. We are goddamn superheroes. We are constantly compared and looked down upon when in reality we should be fed grapes and fanned with palm branches. Don't get me started on the sexual façade we're all supposed to be masters in. I mean, not all women want to twerk their way to an orgasm. Don't live up to the stereotypes! Women can't drive, women can't make more money than men, women can't … women can't … women CAN. Every woman is different, and every woman wants something different. They can't boil us down to stereotypes. We can do whatever the fuck we want to. We can do whatever we want in the bedroom, no questions asked. We are woman, hear us roar.

God is a woman. I truly believe it. I have my reasons, many of which include the fact that our bodies endure a lot more than men's. Our monthly menstrual cycle, childbirth, breastfeeding, you know what I'm talking about – you're living it. Women are powerful creatures, a gift from God herself. We were given these powers so we could run the world. For fuck's sake, we bleed for a week once a month. And we're FINE!? That shit ain't right. So, whenever you start to doubt yourself, or your love life, just remember who created it to begin with.

SUMMARY

Don't forget just how powerful you are as a woman. We have the strength, the endurance, and the passion to keep fighting for what we want. And we know what we want. Letting others cloud our judgement is something that all of us struggle with. We try to make everyone else happy, because we feel that if they're happy, we will be, too. That's not always the case. Listen to yourself and put yourself first. You never know what wonders can happen once you start to live life powerfully.

THE CHARACTER

Every individual has a unique personality. That personality impacts everything they do. The choices we make may seem meaningless to someone else, but everyone is hardwired to care for different things, to be motivated by different things and to work toward different goals. Each choice is like a street we choose on our journey. A man who I consider a main pit stop on one of these many side streets is the one I refer to as "The Character". He has an egotistical, loud personality with a friendly face and a heart of tainted gold. The type of man you would consider The Character has many flattering attributes, from his looks, to his carefree way of movement. It doesn't matter how you meet The Character; just know he will come into your life whether you're ready for it or not. It usually starts off sweet, a tasteful friendship that ends up being just as destructive as a hurricane. The calmness before the storm is exciting, new and almost perfect; but when that baby hits, everything goes into a whirlwind of crazy emotions and thoughts. Trying to explain how or why The Character is the way he is is like trying to explain how water tastes.

The Character is a charming, stupid-funny type of man. This man is the first on my call out list. He will forever be embedded in your brain. Even if you find The One and settle down, there will be instances where this character of a man will dig his way back into your frontal brain. These memories can be sweet and salty. I could sit here and guide you to steer away from The Character because he will tear the beating heart right out of your chest and squeeze the last moments of your life in his bare hands. However, by saying that I wouldn't be realistic with my advice. The lessons I've learned from this type of man are irreplaceable. This was the man who molded me to be the woman I am today. His carefree, childish way of viewing life ended up igniting the womanhood inside of me. Even though I still think of this man often, I'm grateful for his mistakes and the way he mistreated me in the end. Crazy, right? But it's true. Like a Thanksgiving speech, I'm thankful for The Character for many reasons. The most important one being, he helped me see that true love is possible, and he helped me understand how to care for and nurture that love. Instead of dismissing your history with this type of a man, embrace the moment and in the future when looking back, laugh and turn the page because he is just the beginning.

It starts off almost like a fairytale, the man shining before your eyes speaks words that will hypnotize you. His thoughtfulness with strike you as kind and gentlemanly, but every gentleman has flaws. Offering to pick you up and smooth talking you into a special one-on-one cheap date are his specialties and the romance doesn't stop there. You're blinded by the attention and the thrill of a new relationship with a man who seems to be so intriguing and thirsty for you and the pure love you have to offer. You find yourself willing to do things you've never considered, and I'm not speaking sexually. I'm referring to those moments when you want to surprise him at work or meet him somewhere random for a quick chat. This type of man is known for staying put and getting what he wants when he wants it. I guess you can say he's not really a go-getter, more of a wait-and-have-my-desires-fall-into-my-lap type of man. But let's say you don't mind going out of your way because he's such a hard worker and you're blinded by the strong emotional connection you have with him. The very first thought that pops into your head is the decision you will most likely go with. But I want to challenge you to always take the extra moment to think about if that is really the best decision. It's intoxicating to be in this type of love, but the heat can't last forever. You have to both be willing to put in the work. So, let him come to you, especially if you've already gone out of your way for him.

He's an entitled type of man. He takes advantage of your generosity, and he won't put in the same amount of work you do. It almost seems enough, but it doesn't take long for The Character to screw that up. He doesn't think things through, he's in the moment and boy does he look good in that moment.

My personal interactions with this type of man started with The Character I'll call Al. These interactions are distributed across 16 years, and in many different locations. We met by accident through mutual friends when I was only 12 years old. Friends forever, best friends in fact. He was living in New York City and I was living in Florida, often visiting the Big Apple. We stayed connected every minute of every day through texts, phone calls, and our ever-so-famous nightly skype chats. This man made me smile and laugh more times in my life than I ever had before. I was only 12 when we met, 15 when we started our Skype dates, and 16 when we had our first kiss. I was in New York close to four times a year, every year, for seven years. We had conversations that were so silly I barely remember them, but most were so deep and heartfelt that just thinking about it brings me back to a place I haven't been in a long time. Al and I spent nights walking along the Coney Island boardwalk, or the streets of Manhattan. We would meet after he got out of work down in the Union Square subway, and ride the train together to Brooklyn, sharing our day and any thought that came to mind. I was love struck, and whenever I would have to return to the Sunshine State, he would meet me somewhere along the way to the airport to say goodbye. One white winter, I jumped out of my friend's car and met him on a random corner somewhere in route to JFK International Airport. The snow was coming down so hard, our fingers and noses froze within seconds. I can still remember his big blue eyes staring down at me, a slight smirk on his face, when he slowly intertwined his fingers with mine.

"Don't leave," he said.

"I have to," I replied.

One handful of words was all we exchanged. We stared at each other for what felt like years. Smiling, hugging and then I had to go. The lights of the city reflected off his baby blue eyes, his smile mirroring back at me. That's when he leaned in, giving me the most romantic kiss of my life. He swept me off my feet, literally, and spun me around.

"I'll miss you," he whispered.

Denying the fact that I was head over heels for this man, and I was seconds away from refusing to return home, I flashed my smile that had him hooked from the first day and ran to the car. The full story between Al and I is a novel long, full of emotions and false hope. In the end, I was left heartbroken, unfixable, and determined to never love again. Now it's 16 years after we first met and I still feel as if I'm missing a piece of myself, of my heart. They say your first love is always different. Whoever "they" are, they are right. I've never felt that way about someone since, felt a connection as strong and fun as the one I had with The Character but, in the end, it didn't matter what I did, said or tried. I was just another chapter in this man's book and unfortunately it changed me forever.

I spent days fantasizing about him, and nights wishing I were with him. Most of our relationship was strictly friendly. After knowing him for 4 years, we decided to make it official. I was 16 years old, and it lasted all of two months. A summer loving that lasted while I was in New York. The weekend I returned to Florida, I went to the beach to watch the sunset and that's when it all came crashing down. Much like the waves in front of me. I had tried calling him numerous times that day, with no such luck. When the sun was finally starting to set, my phone rang. He was working, hadn't been able to answer my calls, but he missed me too much to talk about it. I hurt him by leaving and he wished I could come back. Drunk in love, I believed him. It broke my heart hearing how I hurt him by not being there for him physically. I expressed my innermost feelings, telling him that no matter the distance, I would be there for him emotionally and that I would be back in his arms in two months.

He threw me off my game so hard, I should have seen it sooner. By that evening I was at my cousin Samantha's house, still drunk in love, telling her all about my trip, all about Al, and how we connected. My first ever physical connection with someone. Then, yet again, the phone rings. I answer, it's Al, his voice trembling saying we need to talk. I knew right then and there that I had made the biggest screw up I could have ever made. I gave myself to a man who waited not even a full weekend to break it off once I was gone from his physical radar. Trying not to make a scene, I tried to tell him that I'd be back in only two months. He didn't want to hear it. He acted as if I had done something wrong, and that I broke his heart. He refused to see our situation for what it was. He wasn't getting his way, and I had to pay the price. The Character is a selfish man, always was and always will be. He only cares for his physical needs versus your emotional needs. Physical wounds can heal but emotional damage takes a lot longer than one would like to admit. I ate shit from him with that very brief phone call. I couldn't believe that, just like that, it was over.

As originally promised, I was back in New York City two months later. Now my phone was blowing up, Al couldn't stop calling and texting. He missed me, he made a mistake, he needed to see me. His charming personality and sexy voice got the best of me. I allowed him one interaction so we could discuss matters like adults, and sure enough, I let him back into my life just as fast as he left it. Yet again, everything was amazing. We were back to our date night rituals, in the dark movie theatre, his hands where they didn't belong. My hands following his lead. We had numerous beach trips together, sun-struck and love-struck all at once. I could seriously see myself with this man forever. He made me so happy. He would playfully pick me up at the beach and twirl me around, throw me in the water, and then save me. Our interactions were always full of passion no matter what we were doing. Like a vicious cycle though, he would destroy it every single time. Whenever I had to go back to reality, he would break things off, hurting me over and over again, each time more than the last. I was stupid enough to think that things could change, that he could change. It's still so hard to believe that we didn't work out. We were great together. We were into the same things. I looked forward to his goofy ways every second of every day. I loved the way he wanted me. The way he would look at me with passion in his eyes. The desire pouring out of him like a broken fire hydrant. I couldn't get over that feeling of being desired by someone so full of character. He had me jumping at his every beck and call. Without hesitation or thinking, I was there. No matter what he needed or where he wanted me to go, I didn't pause for even a second.

Al worked as a doorman in a fancy hotel in New York City, a job perfect for The Character types. I would be in the middle of a serious shopping day in SoHo with my girls, when he'd text me a cute kissy face picture and have me hopping in the first—most expensive—taxi to get to him. Never did he offer to pay for those taxi rides. I never realized it then, not until it was too late. The effort I was giving this man, the love I was expressing and the actions I was taking to make him happy, was all unreciprocated. I literally gave him everything I had, and then some. He put the effort in maybe twice in the 16 years, and that's being generous. He never took a taxi spur of the moment to come see me. If I needed him, he would only show up if it were convenient for him. The one time I broke it off with him he did actually travel across half the city to get to me, but he showed up with a hickey on his neck. Thinking I'm an idiot, he told me he scratched himself. The summer before, he'd left me a neck full of them. I clearly knew what they looked like, from the master himself. His response, instead of telling me the truth, resulted in lying and purchasing an overpriced rose from a lady selling flowers on the street. As love-struck as I was, even that didn't stop the end from coming. After that I couldn't trust him, which eventually led to me not trying. When a woman stops trying with this type of a man, it will only last so long. That's because without you trying so hard, bending over backward, he won't pick up the slack.

So, what do you do when you come across a man who fits the description of The Character? You don't give in to his needs. We all understand that a relationship is a two-way street and requires work from both parties. But a relationship with The Character will be all you unless you put your foot down. Let him come to you when he wants the random meetings or late-night hookups. Don't cater to his every need because once this man gets what he wants and he gets bored, he's striking you out and going to find his home run elsewhere. I want to take this moment to emphasize what I just said. Do not come running at his beck and call, it will backfire and most likely be the demise of your relationship. I wish someone had given me this advice. Maybe my first love and I would be happy ever after if someone had. If you don't follow my advice, just know The Character's all about fun and games, but when it comes down to getting serious, whether it's a conversation or your actual relationship, he's going to make like a turtle and hide in his shell until you back off. That's him in black and white, no sugar coating or rainbow painting the facts that lie before you.

The interactions I've mentioned with The Character make him seem romantic, charming and perfect. That is far from the truth. The first official date he had taken me on was in Times Square, and it was a total disaster. I should have known to run far and fast, but I made the mistake of sticking like glue. He brought me to the McDonalds down the street from the movie theatre, which isn't the bad part. If a man is right for you, it shouldn't matter how he wines and dines you, what matters is the company. Instead, he sat across from me with a mouthful of McChicken and we barely exchanged a few sentences. I refused to eat, mostly because of nerves, and because I couldn't fathom the idea of downing a whole Big Mac in front of him. After our short dinner, we headed over to the movies. We barely watched the movie because The Character is the type of man that is very physical, probably why we barely exchanged any actual words prior to the movie. I fell for it. The movie was great, our form of communication during wasn't bad either, but this still wasn't the worst part. After the movie was over, we headed to Bryant Park to sit at a small metal table, finally starting to loosen up and joke with one another, when it started to get dark. We decided to call it a night and headed for the subway. This man did not have $4.50 to pay for the ride home. We were stuck in Manhattan with no money and no form of transportation. I was in disbelief. I was scared and mad. He did not have a single person to call to pick us up, or maybe he didn't want to call anyone because I was his dirty little secret for over five years (I was between the age of 12-17). It was up to me to figure out a way to get home. I called the one person I knew would come get us, and ironically, he shared the same name as Al. I walked a short distance away to call a former beau of mine who was still obsessed with me. I was embarrassed to tell him the truth in front of my date, so I needed a minute of privacy. Over the phone, I expressed to Al The Second, how my date Al had no money to get us back to Brooklyn, and we needed a ride. After hearing him laugh for what felt like an hour, he asked me where I was and said he would be there in 20 minutes. I hung up, walked back to Al, and told him we had a ride coming. This man did not even apologize for miscalculating his funds and leaving us stranded in a city where we both had nowhere to stay. Once my friend Al The Second pulled up in his Range Rover, I told my date I would give him a signal when I was ready for him to join us. I ran across the street, hopped in the front seat and was ready to leave The Character behind. Mentally, I was fighting with myself, like an angel on one shoulder and a devil on the other, debating whether or not I should leave him. Al The Second was yapping in my ear in the meantime, laughing and saying he couldn't believe that I had gotten myself in this situation. I laughed back, nervously, and then damning my conscious I asked if we could give the poor sap a ride as well. He agreed, after all, Al The Second would have done anything for me. I did not move from the front seat, I did not look up, when I introduced the two I made it quick and the rest of the ride the two Als talked while I pretended to be busy on my sidekick.

After we got to our destination, Al's house, we dropped him off and I said a fast goodbye from the front seat. I barely looked at him, I barely even said bye. I couldn't stop thinking that if I had actually eaten something for dinner, we wouldn't have even had money for the movies. Then I started thinking, if he didn't eat three McChickens we might have had just enough to get back home. There were so many thoughts and doubts running through my mind that I couldn't enjoy the thrill of our first date. Instead, my date ended with me being driven home by a good friend. We jammed to Lil' Wayne's newest CD, made a pit stop by the water to reflect on what had just happened, and then Al The Second drove me home. I told him that evening I owed him big time, and unfortunately, I never got the opportunity to pay him back.

For The Character, you're special but they're not ready. Or so you like to think. A woman's reality versus a man's reality are like two different galaxies. When it comes to The Character's mentality it's all fun and games until the situation gets real. If you get crazy eyes or love on the brain, it's a total turn off for them and makes them run for the hills. They'll shake you off in a casual, smooth, humorous way and you won't even notice that it happened until weeks or even months later when you realize there's no going back to what once was. Even if you don't get all lovey-dovey with him, but you two start to get close in an emotional way, a siren goes off in his head that it's time for a change and off he goes. There's even a possibility that once he ends the relationship, eventually he comes back. He had his fun somewhere else, most likely saw your social networking page or came across an old message and he will contact you. He'll act as if nothing ever happened, and you just might be okay with it because you'd also rather act as if nothing ever happened than remind him of why he left. That could work, and if it doesn't, you could always twist it and say you were playing him back, but we all know what your real intentions were. Those intentions you have or had won't work, plain and simple, don't bother.

Al put me in this situation the first half of our relationship. We were together and sitting on a park bench in Central Park when he exposed his feelings. Less than a year after our first kiss, he confided in me that he was freshly out of a bad relationship with Daisy, a woman he loved. She had left him to go to another country and marry a man she'd never seen in person. She was using Al, and I honestly believe that she was the reason he ended up being so screwed up. She broke his heart, and he couldn't move on from that. It resulted in a destructive series of events for him and his future relationships, which sadly included me. As I listened to him, I couldn't help but feel like I wanted to fix him, I wanted him to love me and I wanted him. After a few weeks, we became so close I felt like I would eventually marry this man. That's when he started to pull back, he dumped me, and his excuse was that Daisy ended up not leaving the country and they wanted to give it another shot. That didn't last long, maybe a month, and I'm being nice. Once Daisy gained light on his new relationship with me, because yes, I took him back after that, she made my life hell. She spread rumors about me to everyone and anyone that knew me, him, my family, his family, whoever. She said all kinds of nasty things about me, all untrue. She even began prank calling me and threatening me over the phone suggesting some very illegal things if I didn't break up with Al. She then began getting her cousin to call me, talking crazy about how I have been prank calling Daisy and saying nasty things. After about two months of this, while on the phone with Daisy and her cousin, I explained that she needs to get over Al because she blew it. I told them that I have better things to do and that prank calling is very elementary. I was out of the house from 5 in the morning until 7 at night, I had no time for her nonsense. While on the line, they put me on hold, came back a minute later, and started apologizing. Apparently, there was someone impersonating me and they were prank calling Daisy on my behalf. Pathetic. All for a man, who eventually turned out to be the biggest loser. After that, the phone calls faded, and I honestly forgot all about Daisy and her childish ways until I started writing this book. Al never got back with her, but his heart never completely healed.

If you end up deciding you want to have fun and games with this sort of man, I'm all for it. If you can turn around and play him like a fiddle the way he did you, more power to you. It might sound crazy, but if you have that chance to make him sing and dance the way you want him to, control his mind and body the way he did with you, take that chance and enjoy every second of it. When do you officially give up? When your heart says its time, when you've gotten that closure every woman wants. Closure can be just as mind-boggling as love itself, but women want what they want and it's usually answers. By that time, it'll be easy to walk away and not look back. You will be able to end that phone call or walk away from that conversation because your heart and mind are officially on the same page.

A personal encounter between the character and I, and when I officially got what we will say is "closure", was over five years after the relationship had been declared dead, 10 years after I met him. We had both moved on, lived separate lives, and had not been in contact for the full five years. This sorry excuse for a man decided that he would find me via social media and express his undeclared love for me. In the 13 years of knowing him, he never once told me that he loved me. After taking my innocence, he insulted me and insisted he wasn't my first. Even after crawling back to him post several awful relationships, he never admitted his faults, or his feelings. And then five years later, this man declares his love for me, expresses his faults, his guilts, his feelings and his sorrow for marrying the wrong woman. I sat there with a fresh glass of sangria, pitcher on hand, repeating every word to my gal pal who sat across from me. As much as I was laughing, and how many glasses I had to drink after this conversation, I felt a calm sense of jitters.

How can you have calm jitters? That's what The Character does to you. He makes you insane in the membrane, feeling emotions that have never been described or defined by the living human race. I'm happy to announce that on that day, the tables had turned. This man I had hoped and prayed would express himself to me, was finally doing it, and I sat there not only in disbelief, but feeling pity for this man. I felt sorry for his wife, who was pregnant during this unwanted encounter. I also felt sorry for him. Sorry that he did not know how to express himself before it was too late, before he threw away something that could have been. But with a smile on my face, I simply replied, "I loved you from the moment I saw you. I carried you in my heart for as long as I could. You disrespected the love I had to give and broke my heart. After all these years, I'm finally happy. Go home to your wife and love her like you've never loved her before." I then blocked his profile and erased all traces of this cartoon character from my life.

There are no exact words to describe the complexity of The Character except for maybe "in the moment". The Character is spontaneous and does whatever feels right from one second to the next. It can be exhilarating and feel like he has the whole world figured out. But once you overcome that stage you realize that he was just a small part of the bigger picture that's about to come. I'm not saying you will forget the guy; you may think of him from time to time but there's a pretty good chance you won't want to. In the beginning, you'll probably be confused as to why he is the way he is, then that confusion will turn to sadness. You might lose your womanly mojo along with a little self-confidence, but once that sadness fades like night into day, you might become angry. Filled with anger toward this man who played you and hurt you. During this anger phase is usually when the woman gets back at him and plays the game right back, because everyone knows how dangerous a woman can be when she's angry. After the anger and games, you're back to your normal happy-go-lucky self, and good for you when you reclaim yourself. I faced all of these phases when it came to Al. The day I made it official and moved to New York, I got a phone call from the one and only. He wanted me to know that he was getting married in the morning. My heart rose to my throat, my hands and legs went numb. My being literally came out of itself, I had an out of body experience. I was watching myself on the phone, listening to mumbles of "I'm sorry", and whatever other nonsense came out of his mouth. After a minute of silence, he said my name. I simply smiled, as if he could see me, and said congratulations. Now his response—I've never been so offended—but here we go. His response was that he missed me and that I should come to his wedding because he'd love to see me. I couldn't believe my ears. I could not fathom the fact that the man I had loved for so long, and so hard, was

1. Telling me he misses me the day before his wedding

2. Marrying another woman, and

3. Inviting me to his wedding.

Not only did I laugh, I fashionably refused. I explained that he should not have been contacting me the day before his wedding expressing his desire for me, how he missed me and wanted me to attend his wedding, to watch the man I thought I would forever love vow his forever love to another woman. And by the way, this woman ended up being my father's best friend's daughter. I expressed, in anger, how wrong he was to do this. Not only to me, but his faithful wife-to-be. As calmly as possible, and this is verbatim, I told him, "I don't want to take the thunder from your wife on her wedding day, she doesn't need to watch her husband desiring another woman on the first day of your forever marriage."

Now, I'm not too proud that I included his innocent wife in my anger-filled RSVP; however, as a woman, we all know that we don't normally respond as perfectly as possible when under stress. This was stressful. My point had been made, I declined as respectfully as I could, and I spent the next two months hurting more than ever now that my chances with my first love were forever done and gone.

We all know that The Character has tendencies to screw up. Whether it's in his daily activities, or when it comes to a female companion. This man can lie, he can cheat, and he can twirl you around that finger of his until you're so dizzy you don't remember your own name. Of course, that only happens if you let him. As I've stated, The Character tends to claw his way back into your life whether you want him to or not. Most recently, I found this man knocking on the door to my life. Stupidly, I answered. Yet again, his wife was pregnant; he couldn't be unhappier. He stated he didn't contact me for a "sob session" but that's exactly what it turned out to be. Like a broken record this man poured his heart out to me, confessing his lifelong regret of disowning me and settling down with the wrong woman. I asked him why he kept getting her pregnant. He responded that he was in a drunken state. This is The Character. He refuses to take responsibility for his actions and continues to stray from home. As much as I cared for this man a long time ago, I just keep coming to the realization that I seriously got lucky. He did me the biggest favor in the world because if he's so quick to turn on his wife, why wouldn't he do that to me? A 30-something-year-old man, still playing the 18-year-old games. That is the way of The Character. For any woman who has settled down with this type of man, best of luck and keep your intuition in check. If your womanly powers are telling you that he's up to no good, just remember Al and his very pregnant wife. The idea of you and him might be enticing, but it's best to leave the water under the bridge. The reality of The Character is never as good as the idea of him.

SUMMARY

Settling down with a man of this breed will lead to a life of constant wondering and questioning. You don't want to be with a man who never fully puts you or your kids first. He's the type that refuses to post you on his social media. There will be a constant feeling like he's hiding something, which more than likely he is. The Character is never satisfied, that's because he has never felt self-satisfied. This man has yet to find his own destiny, to discover his true passions. He's living unfulfilled and hoping that any woman he puts under his belt will lead to this. This is not the case, and this is not the type of man you want. He is sneaky, and downright dirty. The Character tells you what you want to hear yet acts in a selfish manner. The good times and bad times, when compared on a scale, are about the same. The good feels more sensational than the bad, you even forget the horrid moments you've experienced because he is quite the charmer. He's the type that, when all is said and done and you find yourself thinking of him, all you can do is smile. After all, he is The Character.

This type of man changes you forever.

THE SWEETHEART

Another faint memory of a man who I'm going to call out is the one that I call The Sweetheart. An average woman rips through that phase of "bad" boys for an immeasurable amount of time. But what happens to those of us who get sick of that type of a man? Our heart settles for The Sweetheart. Every person is different, and some women might be a great match with a man who is a sweetheart. But what I'm talking about in this chapter is the man you go after because you think you should be with that type of man, not because you actually like him. The man you know you would never really go for if you were in the right state of mind. He's the rebound type of man. The man you go to because he's the opposite of the man who just broke your heart. He's sweet and doting and never forgets an anniversary but there just isn't a spark.

I personally was with a man like this, we can call him Sosa. What he and I had was frustrating and forced. A constant debate we had in literature class in school was that of free will vs. fate. I normally would never categorize this educational debate with a barbaric topic such as love and relationships, but here I go. Fate was with Al, and free will was with Sosa. I couldn't stop the force of the universe from putting me with Al, but I willingly and forcibly threw myself onto Sosa. Much like a teenager enduring high hormones, which at the time I was, I pursued the passion of free will and decided to make my own future with a man who ended up being beyond wrong for me. I ignored every sign that I should not enter a relationship with someone categorized as The Sweetheart. It was never in my nature, never supposed to happen, and because every individual in this universe has the option of free will, I challenged the universe and failed miserably.

The Sweetheart is an acquired taste, and I never cared much for sweets. Vodka, maybe. This brief encounter will forever be implanted in my brain and my heart. I may not have truly loved this kid, but I truly love the insight I gained from being with him. The love he showed me, the respect, the endless times he was there for me, even when I didn't want him to be. He was the perfect transition after the heart-breaking Character type. I hate that I used him, but I was young and didn't know what I was doing. Looking back, he tried to save me from myself. I had become a different kind of person after Al, losing all the qualities that had once made me, me. The innocence of my heart was tainted and torn, and Sosa tried to mend that. He did whatever he could to ensure that I returned to my loving self. What he didn't know, and what I recently realized, is that after a heart wrenching situation as that with Al, you can never be who you were before. I was going through PTLD, Post Traumatic Love Disorder. I doubt that's a real medical diagnosis, but it should be. A woman scorned from love is destined to change. Mentally, emotionally, even physically, you become a different person. The universe tested me with fate versus free will and whether or not I passed, I will never know. What I do know, is that even though The Sweetheart wasn't meant to be my forever man, he was the perfect transition after a broken heart. He is the type of man that gives women like me the strength to keep on keeping on. Now, Sosa is doing great things for himself, and even though he has yet to find love, he has learned to love himself. Which is something neither of us knew how to do while we were together. The free will of choosing to be together was a disaster, but the fate that we both came out stronger because of it, that was destiny.

There are women in this world that are made for men such as The Sweetheart, who will have long, happy marriages with this type of man. However, if you're the type of woman who is looking for a real-life romantic comedy, look elsewhere. This faithful, sweet and pathetic type of man is hard to find and is only suitable for a certain type of woman. I use the word pathetic, because well, that was Sosa's favorite word.

I met Sosa at the beach when his cousin was trying to pick me up. His cousin was that of The Character, so I strayed from my usual ways and decided I'd take the safer route with The Sweetheart. I stayed mentally and emotionally faithful, and happy, for all of two months. After that, it was a constant see-saw of breaking up and getting back together. Sosa was always there, waiting like a reliable puppy. I constantly confused the kid and could never just settle down with him. It even got to a point where I was dismissing my own way of life and catering to his. I tried that hard. A good example of this is when my entourage was going out on the town, a fancy strip club in Manhattan. Instead of getting dolled up, hair done and joining my girls for a night of fun, I stayed in with a sick sweetheart, made him tea and watched Family Guy for hours. From the moment my girls closed the door, I knew I made a regretful mistake. Instances like this made this animosity grow inside of me toward this kid who only wanted to love me. Moral of this pathetic short story, is don't go against your gut. Remember that sixth sense and that it's there to save you heartache. Don't ignore it, because in the end you will wish you went to a strip club causing chaos with your crew rather than settling down with the wrong kind of man.

A perfect time in our very short relationship, where I was forcing myself into something that shouldn't be, was my 17th birthday. I did not want Sosa there and he came anyway, bearing a very emotionally attached gift. He had taken my name plate necklace the week before without me realizing it, and was holding it in his small, dainty hands as we stood face to face behind the restaurant where I was celebrating my life on this world. He began to express his innermost feelings with me, "I have never told a girl this, but I care about you so much. I think I love you," he said. Unlike my past emotions with Al, I felt forced. Rather than fate bringing us together, it was my own free will that was forcing me to say the words back to this sappy sweetheart. I looked into his big blue eyes, yes, I had a thing for blue-eyed men, and repeated the dreadful words, "I think I love you, too."

His pale face turned bright red, his beady blue eyes grew with desire, and he pulled me in for a romantic encounter. He turned me around brushed my hair off of my neck and began putting my famous name plate necklace around my throat. I say famous because anyone that knew me knew that this was my signature necklace. I wore it for years at a time never taking it off. This time, when I looked down, I saw something was added on, dangling from the middle of my name. A shiny evil eye charm. My love for the evil eye was, and still is, as strong as ever. I own a handful of items that have the evil eye, and I even have it tattooed on my ribcage, and my inner elbow. But my love for that necklace was stronger than my love for Sosa. As sad as it is to admit that, I was happier to have my necklace back, and even though I love the evil eye and everything it stands for, I was upset that something so dear to me had remnants of him on it now forever. My signature, my personal logo, had been corrupted by an emblem of what should have never been. I put a face on, smiled, and thanked him with a kiss. Fast forward not even three months later, I went camping with my JROTC Army class, and the very first night, the evil eye emblem was ripped from my signature necklace, never to be found again. I believe in the universe, and I believe that was fate. It was only the first of many signs that Sosa and I shouldn't have been in a relationship. I never admitted to him what happened to that charm, but deep down I knew right then it was the end of us. My free will had faded, my desire to make things work blew away in that star filled night around the bonfire, the little love I had for this sweetheart was forever gone, along with the charm.

A confident, strong, independent woman tends to get along better with a man who is just as confident and independent as she is. But even some of the strongest women I know have been drawn in by the idea of

The Sweetheart. He is the type of man who is lighter than a floating feather. His humor is different than any other kind you've ever heard; it's more of that innocent humor that you eventually label as corny. Even his looks are softer than your average man, he doesn't impress, or even try for that matter. He's sincere with who he is and either you accept him or you don't, but regardless of what you choose he will always accept you no matter what faults you may portray. I messed up more times than you can count in the almost year we were together. I would stray to my old ways with The Character we know as Al. I would even dig deep into my past, leaving Sosa with his entourage to go and see old flames. Don't get me wrong, it wasn't anything physical with these other men, it was all mental, emotional and wrong. My desire to find an independent man was stronger than ever and this poor, sweet kid was suffering for my indecisive actions. I hurt him more times than I could count and, almost 10 years later, Sosa has yet to find another girlfriend after me. Feelings of regret and disappointment overwhelm me whenever I think of Sosa and I wish I had never lured him into my world. I was wild, daring, adventurous and loud. He was the opposite, and we all know the saying that opposites attract; but very rarely does it work out.

Many, and I mean many, women who yearn for that good guy who's going to treat her right and love her to the moon and back would kill for a man like this. When they get with The Sweetheart, it's all love and fun until time passes you by and you end up staring at this man and being annoyed with what's in front of you. You want him to have a strong opinion. You want him to sweep you off your feet, do something dramatic and passionate. You want him to be independent. But you'll be standing there thinking to yourself, "What am I doing with him, why did I ever start this, why is he so nice... why, why, why?" Unless you're the type of woman who loves to be clingy and who's all for repetition in your relationship, call him out and be done with it. He is too nice! You end up being the man in the relationship, which at first might be exciting and new, but ladies please, let him be the head to call the shots and you continue to be the neck to turn him where he needs to go. If you find yourself there staring at him with disgust, it's not because his looks are repulsive, it's because he isn't what you're looking for. Yes, of course you can wait around for him to change but get real! That's the way he has always been and what makes you think you can change him? People don't change major personality traits, they can attempt, but we are who we are. In a situation like that you're better off parting ways and eventually if it's meant to be, it will be. If you're at all independent or outgoing, this man is probably not for you. Do him a favor, save his heart, and let him go.

Be honest with yourself. If you're lying to the poor guy's face, you're lying to yourself. If you won't do it for him, do it for you. He might be sweeter than sugar itself, more comforting than ice cream, but that situation is a volcano waiting to erupt. Let's say you decide to hold off and see where things could end up. *Maybe it's not that bad, maybe I'm just overreacting, maybe, maybe*, maybe should not be running through your head because those are excuses. Those sorry excuses will be the spark that ignites the explosion, take it from me. The sweetheart will be better off without you, and you will be better off without him.

Years later, after the relationship died and was long since decayed, Sosa managed to find me on Snapchat. At this point I was in a serious, committed relationship to a man Sosa had encountered in the past when we were together. He knew my current beau, and once upon a time, when Sosa and I were a thing, he had even approached my newfound love asking him for directions on the subway. Fast forward to our current conversation and realizing all the pain I had caused this kid, I decided not to tell him how happy I was. How successful I had become, or how very pregnant I was. Instead, I learned from my past mistakes, those feelings of regret when it came to this sappy love interest, and informed him that life was good, I was happy for his current situation and that I wished him the best. I informed him that it wasn't the best idea to contact me anymore because I didn't want to hurt him again, refusing to give this sweetheart any false hope. We ended the very brief conversation and I deleted him from my friends list. Sosa had been through enough, he didn't need to see still images or short video clips on the life he could have had with me. I will forever reflect back on Sosa, wishing that things could have been different, especially for his sake. Unfortunately, that's life, people use, abuse and reuse. I had finally found the courage to let him go, emotionally letting him fly free to a life that he can appreciate and love versus a fake love life with me.

SUMMARY

When it comes to this type of a man, it's usually best to leave him alone. Don't try to change your desires to fit what you think you need. Try to listen to the sixth sense in the back of your head instead. The Sweetheart was sensitive, overbearing and just a little too much for me. I have learned now to not try to make my own fate, it only came back to bite me later.

THE MISTAKE

We all make mistakes, some bigger than others. And many women end up with men who are just that, mistakes. My encounter with The Mistake was by accident, and I told myself I would not get involved, nor touch him with a 10-foot pole. However, being across the country, in a developing country for that matter, made him look better than he really was. The Mistake had huge emotional damage that his family had caused, and at that point in my life, everyone else's damage looked better than my own. I mistakenly got involved, and it makes me want to throw up every time I think of him. Ladies, there are emotionally damaged men out there who will project that damage on you. Stray far, far away whenever you encounter someone like this. Do not feel the need to fix him or help him. He's a big boy and will figure it out without you. Overall, The Mistake is a type of man that will drag you down. He comes with a lot of emotional baggage, an aura that is full of hate and hurt, and a personality that is as dull as a blank book. You cannot fix it, nor can you change his life. He will be miserable as long as he chooses to be and will only bring you down.

The Mistake I got involved with lasted two months, the length of my time in Europe. Those were the longest two months of my life. They still feel as if it were two years and not two months. We were both 17 and this man, who I will call Mer, was the saddest, most soul-draining man I have ever met in my life. And I've met a lot of men. The encounter between us started at a local bar where I found myself every Friday and Saturday night. It was the only bar that would play American music, so naturally that's where I ended up. He sat alone at the end of the bar with a full bottle of vodka, yes, my ultimate favorite poison. He saw me bopping to the music, alone, with my table full of empty vodka glasses. We were both seventeen. Much like a strong man, I can hold my liquor, but much like a woman, I can't refuse free liquor. He came over with his expensive bottle, offering to share. Mer then began telling me his whole sad life story. We sat there, music in one ear, Mer's monotone voice in the other. He felt connected to me apparently because he didn't spare any details. His brother was the favorite of the family, had a lot going for him, and Mer and his brother never really had the best relationship. A year prior to our encounter, Mer's brother videotaped a very graphic motion picture that included his gruesome suicide, on Mer's birthday. Hence why he was on a Euro trip without his family, probably trying to find himself. My natural womanly instincts made me feel pity for this man, almost creating a physical attraction. It could have been the vodka, that wouldn't surprise me because you know, when in Europe, right? However, I felt the need to fix this poor soul. I wanted to give this man a reason to live, I didn't need to see on the news that he offed himself because he couldn't live with the guilt. I'm naturally a happy-go-lucky person whose aura seems to attract the neediest of people. And, in that drunken moment, I made the mistake of making a connection with the saddest man I could have ever met.

When I describe Mer as the saddest man, I do not mean that in the slang term like he is the most pitiful man, but rather in the literal sense that he was a very sad, distraught man. The type of man that falls under The Mistake category usually has some sadness to him. But The Mistake is always a man that needs to be fixed, healed or is just flat out crazy. Mer was and most likely still is all those things. This is a type of man that you try so desperately to forget, to push so far back in your mind that he becomes nonexistent. It works the majority of the time, but then there are instances when his slimy being comes to light and you can't help but wince. His family life was dysfunctional, more than most families. He was disliked by friends, and whoever met him, even for a second, felt bad for him. Everything about this type is out of this world. He is almost like a fictional character, made up to bring conflict or horror to a situation. Sadly, this species of men exists in real life, and I seriously see a potential for serial killer status whenever I come across them. The Mistake can be a lifelong regret that will never fade or disappear. No magic in the world can take away the horrific memories you might have shared with this person. There is no fixing this kind of man, unless you're a certified psychotherapist. Even then, are they really fixed? Probably not.

The time when I was with Mer was a desperate time in my life. I offered a listening ear and a shoulder to cry on, and yes, he literally cried on my shoulder. His mood swings were more advanced than that of a woman going through menopause and his way of life was destructive to say the least. After my never-ending two-month experience with Mer, he decided to invite himself to my townhouse in Tampa, Florida. Never did I ever invite this creep to visit the state of Florida, never mind my townhome. He said his flight was booked and would be staying with me for a week. A week from hell. Which actually turned out to be 10 days, because The Mistake is a pathological liar.

I'm not one to deny a person in need. Again, I did not need this weirdo committing suicide, or a horrific crime, under my name. So, even though we were not dating, I allowed this character to stay with me, all while trying to convince him to get a hotel room. His refusal led to my annoyance, and after not even 24 hours I was colder than ice. I was so rude to The Mistake of a lifetime, hoping he would get the picture and make like Houdini and disappear. And just my luck, no such thing happened. Instead, when trying to leave him alone in my townhome while I went down south to visit my family and friends, he tagged along. Now you see, my father was never the type to allow me to have boyfriends, or friends that were boys, but The Mistake was just so miserable, and my dad had heard his sad story and allowed him to stay in the detached mother-in-law suite in his apartment complex. I ended up ditching him for the remainder of his trip, leaving him alone in the suite to fend for himself while I went and partied with my friends, and had an unforgettable evening with a future basketball star. While having the time of my life at a house party, exchanging pearly white smiles with men, my now estranged brother decided to show up with The mistake and ruin everything. My brother informed me that ditching this poor kid was wrong, and that he came to hang out with me, so I had to accommodate him. I decided to liquor up, much like on the Euro trip, and let the sorry sap hang out; after all, he was supposed to get on the next flight home in the morning. Or so I thought.

Carless at the time, because I had a tendency to drive on flat tires, I borrowed my best friend's beater car to drive this insane individual to the airport. As I've previously stated, I'm a big believer in the universe, and with the universe comes karma. Never had I ever experienced instant karma until Mer came storming into my life. After a lifetime of a ride, which usually lasts 30 minutes, we arrived at the departure gate of the airport. I refused to park, I wanted to get this over with, so I had him hop out of the car, barely even braking before he got out. I did not watch him walk away; I did not check to see if he made it in safe. I was free. I blasted the local radio station and kept changing the words to mimic my heart filled feeling that "HE IS GONE," and never will I see him again. At this point, my adrenaline was rushing, I was almost home free, and I could see the only traffic light at the end of the long winding road. Windows down, the breeze blowing my stresses away, I was screaming *I'M FREE!* as loud as I could, when all of a sudden, the front hood of my friend's car came flying up, smashing into the windshield and breaking it into a million pieces. I had glass all over my legs, arms, and hands from trying to hold up the windshield. Within seconds, my phone was ringing, Gollum (also known as Mer) supposedly missed his flight and I had to come back to get him and spend one more never-ending evening with him. One tow truck later, an hour of waiting for my friend's dad to save me, and Mer's monotone voice in my ear saying how happy he was that he could stay with me another evening, I wanted to die. Karma won; the universe made its point.

Ladies, don't ever feel obligated to a man. Fight your natural womanly instincts and do not try to save someone who doesn't want to be saved or doesn't want to put in the work. Save it for the professionals and save yourself. The Mistake was and always will be the most hated time in my life. I learned to hate myself during that time. I was always one for self-love and empowerment but The Mistake sucked the hope out of me and left me with nothing but the taste of vomit in my mouth. I refuse to discuss the moments we shared, kissing or otherwise, because the thought of it brings my stomach to my throat. With this breed of a man, forgive yourself. Don't take this brief time in your life too seriously, and do not reflect on any physical contact you might have had with this person. If you haven't encountered a man of this breed, go out and celebrate with drinks. Don't look across the bar though; keep your eyes on your entourage, or if you're on a Euro trip without them like I was, keep your eyes in your cup. Instead, appreciate your good-heartedness and learn from this, or learn from me. After Mer left for good, I never called. I never texted, and I never followed up. His plane could have crashed or gone missing and I wouldn't know it because I ran far and fast after he got out of my car. Admittedly, he did try to contact me multiple times on various social media platforms, through phone calls, texts, and sappy love letters. I did not respond; I no longer felt bad for him. I refused to try to save him. If he didn't feel bad for ruining my summer, or what was left of my summer when he abruptly came to visit, it proves he has no shame in his game and I shouldn't feel shameful to do the same.

SUMMARY

With every relationship, no matter the type, you learn something. If you don't learn something, you become something. In this regretful experience, there were many things to be learned.

1. Don't go drinking at a bar alone.

2. Don't fall for free booze.

3. If you don't follow 1 and 2, run far and run fast when you screw yourself into befriending what will be the biggest regret of your life.

Not only did I learn these life lessons, but I gained a new personality trait, I became selfish. Post-relationship lessons learned are a given. We can always learn something. But to actually gain a new personal quality that will forever affect your life is rare. Through all the disgust, regret, and effort to depress my memories of Mer, I gained an unforgettable characteristic that leaves me forever grateful. Not to him, god no, but grateful for myself in that I was in a situation I should have never been in, and I was able to take away from that. I'm here giving you all kinds of valuable advice, but one thing I can only express so much is that you control your fate. I became selfish after encountering The Mistake and that is an attribute that has helped me know myself and what I need from relationships better. Ill-advisedly, we all have The Mistake in our lives we wish we could take back, or erase. If you're with him now, listen to your sixth sense and stop listening to his guilt trips. You cannot fix anyone. If you've been with a man like that in the past, stop beating yourself up. Relationships are a two-way street and that type of man takes way more than he gives. You did what you had to do to get out. And if you're thinking of getting involved with someone who sounds like Mer, for god's sake, RUN.

THE BAD BOY

This next type of man is well-known no matter where you're from. The Bad Boy. Almost every woman knows this type, and has encountered, dated, or even married this kind of man. They are dangerously addictive, close to perfection, and considered a natural high. Much like The Character, his personality traits are infectious and beyond desirable. The difference being, The Bad Boy is downright bad. He may be a law breaker, a freak in the sheets, or flat-out dangerous. Women love the chase of a man just as much as men love chasing women. It's a natural force to want what you can't have. When it comes to this series of men, it's hard to hook and keep them. They say if you burn your hand on the stove it teaches you to not put your hands near the burners again. But this is one situation we can't get enough of, no matter how many times we get burned. The Bad Boy always knows the right things to say, knows how to keep things interesting, and loves a good challenge. If you're the type of woman who is easily pursued or an easy catch, well the time frame for you and a bad boy is as long as a fresh breath of air. Quick and easy. If you're the kind of women who plays hard to get, loves a good game, and can multitask your professional personality with a flirtatious one, then your encounter with The Bad Boy should last a bit longer.

The Bad Boy variety, and I've encountered quite a few, is a tough type to play with. You really have to know what you're doing in order to hook one of these. Most women end up with a man like this at some point or another. From adventure seekers to shy, reserved types, all women find themselves wanting a bad boy at one point or another. Like a mosquito can sense a human, we can smell a bad boy from about 164 feet away. Bad boys are typically not the greatest in school, they may be a jock, or usually have high-profile jobs later in life unless they have a criminal background (which is highly possible with this breed of man). In that case, they possess more personable jobs that involve human interaction. You normally won't find a bad boy working in the IT field, for example. One of my gifts, as I've said earlier in this book, is that I can think like a man. This thinking led me to a handful of men that are categorized under this specific genre, and I learned quite a few lessons from all of them.

First, you want to stay on your toes practically all the time. The Bad Boy will constantly throw curveballs at you, and if you want to play the game right, you have to know how to play ball. A good example of this behavior is from one of the first Bad Boys I met in my life, and I'll call him Tito. This man had my mind running in a million different directions trying to figure out what it was he wanted. He wanted me, then he didn't, he would call and then he wouldn't answer. He drove me bananas. Needless to say, his indecisive nature cured me of his bad boy aura, and I disappeared on him. Like any other woman, I love a good chase, but not if I'm running forever. This is a common mistake. We get caught up in the chase, thinking that in the end it would be worth it. The likelihood of settling down with a man that you're chasing is slim, give up before you become as skinny as Tito.

He was my brother's friend, and yes, I had a crush on a handful of his friends. That's what big brothers are for, right? I had met Tito before he became my brother's friend on one of my many Euro trips. He pursued me without hesitation. I kept my distance and told myself I wouldn't get involved. One reason being he was a bad boy, the other being he was half my weight. He was constantly getting into brawls with the locals in Gusinje-Plav, a small European village our parents are from in Montenegro, and it turned out he already had a girlfriend. His bad boy ways got the best of me though, and I fell into a small heap of trouble with him. Tito and I lasted about two weeks and I rarely, if ever, think about him. He was just another man that convinced me that The Bad Boy life wasn't for me. Even though this brief encounter was purely emotional, thank god, he taught me that I should always stick to my sixth sense.

Don't give into a man just because he's pursuing you or promising you things. The moment you lay eyes on him and decide you don't want anything to do with him, listen to yourself and don't let yourself look like a fool. The only time I saw Tito after that summer was two summers later when I was spending the week in Staten Island with some cousins. Two brothers, both very good looking and of The Bad Boy variety, came through to pick me and a friend up for a late-night ride. The minute I got in the back seat, looked up and saw Tito, I couldn't help but start hysterically laughing. He immediately turned red like a tomato, not moving his gaze from the dashboard, hoping that this was a nightmare he would wake up from; however, this wasn't a nightmare, but a sick joke from the universe. This joke of a man was sitting inches away from me, and the reality of just how pathetic he was hit me like a ton of bricks. In that instant, I had never been so relieved that I didn't do anything more with this man. The aftershock of when I first met him wore off, and I was seeing him in his true light. He was really not that handsome, or charming. The feeling of happiness struck me like lightning, I had dodged yet another bullet. By this time, I'm a professional dodger because these crazy men should have destroyed me a long time ago. Thankfully, that was the last time I ever had to lay eyes on the scrawny stoner bad boy.

Another lesson I learned from a different Bad Boy encounter came from a boy named Nelly. I'm not talking about the rapper. Nelly was a long-term relationship, and then an on-again-off-again fling. We met in grade school, but our relationship started in high school, after Al and I broke up the first time. I watched this kid who was a straight-A student blossom into an everyday offender. I fell for him, and I fell hard. His bad boy ways were addictive and contagious. After a year of being together, I had professors telling me that we were like water and oil, we would never mix. I was headed down a professional path, whereas he was headed down to the local jail. One trademark Bad Boy experience I had with Nelly was when my family went out of town for two weeks, leaving me alone with the house and car. I had Nelly over almost every other day, never actually allowing him to spend the night, because come on, you have to hook The Bad Boy, not be hooked. As usual, our time together consisted of our usual banter, movie night and dot, dot, dot. However, one night my best friend, Margarita and her Bad Boy boyfriend came to join us for a movie. We had a great time on our double date, and later in the evening my friend's boyfriend (not worth mentioning) went home, leaving the three of us.

It was time to take Nelly home and instead of driving the two main people in my life, I decided to give my friend the wheel. Now, Margarita has been my best friend since the 6th grade. Our friendship is just as strong today, over 12 years later, and this is probably why. She drove my black Mercedes over half an hour to Nelly's house, all the while Nelly and I were committing all kinds of crimes in the back seat. She noticed what was happening when we were at a red light, local county sheriff pulled up next to us, and our car was still bouncing. We could have blamed it on the sound system I had installed, but I'd be lying. Lost in the moment with my current Bad Boy, I heard my friend laughing, asking if she was allowed to turn around and see what was going on. I told her to keep her eyes on the road, and as I am telling her this I look up, see the sheriff on one side, and a limo that had full-blown porn playing on the TV on the other side. That night's police scare was the funniest sign from the universe I could have ever gotten, and luckily no one was arrested. Moral of this story, and the lesson I will never forget, is to never condone sexual activity when in a moving car while pulled up next to a cop. But, if you do, make sure you have a limo advertising adult films on the big screen in the car next to you.

Nelly was my high school sweetheart. We shared many memories, good and bad. I even changed my entire class schedule to mirror his. We were inseparable for quite some time, until I decided I wanted to get back with The Character, Al. I ruined a good thing with Nelly for an unstable relationship with another man. It was worth it in the end; they were both wrong for me. After leaving Nelly high and dry, he refused to talk to me for close to a year. He had found himself another young-and-in-love female to make chaos with and enlisted in the Army. When I heard that, I couldn't believe that this bad boy had signed his life rights away to a military institution. I figured it would benefit him in the long run, hoping it would change him for the better. I was wrong. He was kicked out for reasons I still don't know.

He was your typical Bad Boy, unable to follow the law, and relentless in his ways. This type of man is fun for a while, but women mature faster than men and you'll eventually want to end it before they end you. Don't jeopardize your future for any man. If he loves you, he will make sure he does everything and anything to help you succeed versus holding you down.

The next Bad Boy lesson I learned came from a boy named A.B. What a name, right? Well, A.B. was a long childhood crush of mine, and the chase for this man took close to 10 years, but I did catch him. He ended up being my senior prom date, which was a huge mistake, but the after-party was better than prom. A.B. and I met Dee, another one of my good friends, Dee. That night we decided to go to the beach afterhours with some beer, music and glow sticks. We went through a six-pack and the fun was just starting when we saw flashlights headed toward us. My quick Brooklyn reflexes had me jumping up and throwing all the beer in a nearby bush before I could even think what I was doing. I quickly sat back down, grabbed my energy drink and put it in front of me. After all, I was most definitely underage at this point. Two very manly, very scary police officers come up to us, asking what we were doing on private property.

"Oh, wow, I had no idea, officer. I come here all the time, I didn't know this was private property," Dee explained.

"Have you been drinking?" the big black officer asked.

"I have an energy drink, officer; I don't drink!" I quickly shouted out.

Meanwhile, my vagina of a prom date stood, face down, looking and acting like a mute.

"What did you do with the beer, guys? Don't lie to me. If you tell me the truth, you won't be in trouble, I promise," said the other, a white officer, just as big as the first.

"I threw it in the bush. I'm sorry, I didn't mean to hide it from you, it was a natural reflex," I said as fast as I could, pointing in the direction of the bush.

The big black officer walked over, stuck his hand in the knee-deep bush, and pulled out an 18-pack. Luckily, the six-pack was already drunk and thrown away.

"How old are you kids? Let me see some ID," The two officers said simultaneously, as if they'd rehearsed this before.

We all began to pull out our IDs when I saw bad boy A.B. reaching for his fake one. I quickly grabbed the wallet out of his hands and told the officers he was not 100% normal and pulled out his legal license. I handed mine along with A.B.'s, both IDs showing that we were underage.

"I told you, officer, I've been drinking my energy drink. I didn't have any beer," I said, waving my can of Monster around like a truce signal.

"I had one," A.B. finally spoke.

"Officers, these are all mine, I am of age and brought these crazy kids out here after prom night so they could have some fun in the sand." Dee covered for us.

The officers smiled and threw away the two open cans, then handed us our 18-pack, or what was left of it, anyway. They informed us that we needed to lock it in the trunk of our car and drive straight home. Normally, this is probably super illegal; however, we really did just live down the street. With my hair freshly styled for prom in a half updo, and a t-shirt that exclaimed "I LOVE TO PARTY," I flashed the biggest smile, said thank you, winked, and hopped in the car. Even though my Bad Boy was more of a bad buzzkill that evening, I saved him from going to jail. I saved his future basketball career with one swoop of his wallet. I say this because as it turns out, one parking lot away was A.B.'s best friend. He encountered the same officers right after we drove off, handed them a fake I.D. and landed himself in jail that night. The lesson I learned in this situation is that sometimes a bad boy is a big pussy and you need to take the reins. Otherwise, you're all going to jail.

An update on the infamous A.B. is that he ended up ruining his whole basketball career on his own, without my help. I saved him from one booking, but a few months later he managed to land himself in jail for a more serious offense. The only reason I know this is because after I moved away to New York, and came back to Florida, A.B. contacted me to reconnect. This is one of the many times Google has saved me. What I found was a felony offense for

1. Burglary of occupied dwelling, unarmed, and most surprisingly,

2. Sexual assault of a 12-year-old under special conditions.

I could not believe my eyes or my computer screen. Never will I ever forget my bad boy prom date, and how I dodged yet another bullet.

The last type of bad boy, and unexpectedly the most normal one of the bunch, is the one I call Odell. Odell and Al, The Character are actually related. But Odell is your typical everyday bad boy. He comes from money, he's spoiled, has sex appeal, great style, and is extremely handsome. Despite the fact that years later, I see he's lost his hair, he's still one good looking son of a bitch. Not that his mom's a bitch, she's actually very sweet.

Odell and I grew up in the same neighborhood. I had fantasized about this mystery of a man ever since I knew what a crush was. I had always wanted to taste his lips and knew that one day I would. I just never thought I would have shared more than that, most of which I wish I could forget. It all started when he befriended my brother. The two began hanging out, going out, and becoming the best of bros. My brother made the mistake of inviting me out one night with them, and I brought along Margarita for support. This night is almost forgettable because my fake ID was turning 21 and Margarita and I had way too many free shots. Now, Odell was good-looking and his sex appeal could attract a woman from a mile away, so I watched him throughout the night. I watched him grind with multiple skinny blondes, I saw how he sexually poured vodka down a brunette's throat when the Trey Songz song "Bottoms Up" came on. I even stalked him when he invited a bride-to-be and her bridal party to his V.I.P. suite in a bar. Now remember, with bad boys you have to know how to play the game. As angry as I was on the inside, on the outside I was just happy drunk. Margarita and I went to the outside bar, enjoyed free shots from every angle, danced like there was no tomorrow, and got a few phone numbers from men we would never call.

Once the bar was closing and it was time to leave, we all get into Odell's brand new, off-the-lot Charger. I had complimented and congratulated him on such a fine vehicle earlier that day. Never did I think I would give him a congratulatory gift that he, nor his car, would ever forget. Mistakenly, my brother and Margarita squished me in the middle of the back seat. Halfway home, my body decided that free, not-your-birthday shots were actually cheap vodka and I was starting to reject it. Barely able to keep it in my mouth, I start jumping over Margarita in the backseat of the driver's side, opening the window and barely making it out to release the acetone taste of vodka. I'll skip the gory details, but Odell had to get his car detailed about three times during his stay with us before he could get the stains or smell out. I don't know if it was my charm, my patience, or my desirability (when I'm not spilling my insides out, at least), but I began to notice that Odell was opening up to me. Physically, not so much emotionally. After all, he was a Bad Boy. After another night out with my brother, I decided to get away from Odell's sexual ways with strangers, it was making me crazy. I went out with my girls instead and managed to get home a few minutes before my brother and Odell came back. Odell was bleeding from his knuckles, he had cracked his very expensive watch, and his shirt had been torn. Apparently, when I wasn't there, he was just as messy drunk as I was the first night. He had slipped on the dance floor, fell, broke his watch, knuckles, and managed to tear his shirt when my brother was trying to help him up. Feeling bad for this sexy Bad Boy, I drunkenly went into the kitchen to get him a small bag of ice and some water. By this point, my brother was passed out in the next bedroom. I entered my room, where Odell decided he would be sleeping during his duration at our home (and no I did not sleep in there with him, I do have class). I sat on the foot of the bed and handed him ice, laughing. He started laughing back, telling me that he didn't need ice for his hand, but he needed it for something else. If you know how a man's anatomy works, you'll know he was referring to his private area, because I had apparently aroused him. My lifelong desire to taste this man's luscious lips came to an end that night. Play the game, ladies, and get what you want. I got what I wanted, and then some.

This was one of many encounters that Odell and I had during his two-week stay in my neck of the woods. Another included a hot tub, and his family vacation home which was an hour away from mine. That story starts and ends with strip poker. My emotional infatuation with Odell began after he left to go home. It quickly ended a month later when I made my annual Euro trip and met a young girl who strangely looked almost exactly like me. I'll call her Amanda. I was one week into my trip when I found myself at the American bar that I love so much. I was enjoying my drink and the music when this mirror image of myself came up to me, asking if I was Cindy.

"Yes, do I know you?" I asked.

"No actually, but my boyfriend was just in Florida hanging out with your brother for like two weeks," Amanda responded.

My face must have turned all shades of red, because obviously she was referring to my Bad Boy Odell.

"Oh, you're Odell's girlfriend?" I giggled in return. "Don't worry, sweetie, I took good care of him." I smirked, returning to my drink.

I didn't wait for her response, I turned around and continued drinking, mingling with my entourage that had finally managed to come join me for the summer. Some women might say that was very rude of me, but I had no idea Odell had a girlfriend. It was never mentioned, not even in the slightest form. And this bitch looked like she could have been my twin. Same hair style, color, height, weight. For god's sake, even a friend of mine went up behind her and grabbed her hair playfully, thinking it was me. Odell was a Bad Boy, and this is what Bad Boys do. They hide the fact they're in relationships, because, according to Amanda, they were together for two years. Two years, and he was so quick to flirt like he had never seen a woman in his life. But it does also explain how, during that night of strip poker, he couldn't get it up.

SUMMARY

All in all, The Bad Boy type is fun, but dangerous. They're of a breed that includes the most handsome men in the world. They know what to say, how to say it, and what to do to woo you. Most women would have probably fallen apart post Odell and his straying ways. I learned from it. As if he were my sensei, I learned from the master. I absorbed all his Bad Boy ways and twisted them to become my own. For the sake of my heart, I had to learn. I had to master, and I had to put it into action.

Bad boys are tempting. My advice is to tune into your sixth sense and listen to yourself. If you can see a future with this type of man, go for it, but if he's just stringing you along for the ride, cut him loose and run for the hills.

ME, MYSELF AND I

Aside from knowing the characteristics of the different types of men, to eventually find the right one for you, you need to learn how to love yourself. After all the Characters, Sweethearts, Mistakes and Bad Boys, I found myself feeling stuck. I couldn't fathom the idea that I had yet to find The One and that I kept screwing up my life with these pathetic encounters with these types of men. Granted, for the most part, I was having fun, but on the other hand it was making me hate myself. I was becoming these men. These lessons I was learning and applying were changing me. I felt myself regressing, bending to their ways instead of creating my own. Spiritually, I was feeling negative; physically, I was gaining weight; and educationally, I was beginning to fail. I had let myself go. I had given up and could not figure myself out. Life seemed so big and was so hard, and I couldn't figure out which way to go to fix it. My life came to a standstill. Like sitting water, no ripples or waves to move me along. I was a floating duck. An ugly duckling waiting to transform into a beautiful swan.

How can you progress and move forward when you're stuck in the past? Have you ever felt like your mind is stuck? You're going through the motions of the present, going through your everyday routine, but your brain is always in rewind. You try to get away from it. You find things that are completely different from what you're used to, meet and befriend people you normally wouldn't, say and think things that are completely and insanely out of this world, but your thoughts can't help but go back to that place. It's a weird, pitiful, deep, hopeless feeling. The kind of feeling you get when you've lost someone close to you or broke something extremely valuable to your heart. For an outsider looking at your life, it may not make sense why you're feeling so depressed. You have things you couldn't have ever imagined having, you keep picturing how almost perfect things are going and how extraordinary they'll be in the future; but why do you keep letting your mind wander back in time? Why is it that whenever you feel you're at your peak, you bring yourself back into the deepest pit of misery? People say that you are your own worst enemy, and I can see the truth behind that. However, has anyone ever stopped to think that maybe it's not you who's your enemy, but your past? That question might seem quite absurd to most, but if you stop to think about it, I think you'd find a greater meaning behind it all. Your past is what makes you who you are today but dwelling in that era and letting it control you is an extremely powerful, dangerous thing. You can ruin everything you have going for you all because you can't let go, you can't move on, you can't escape the idea of what used to be, what used to exist. What do you do then? That's just another mystery in life every person has to work through to get to their fate. You are what you make of yourself and as funny as it sounds, I think the past shouldn't matter and that even though things happen for a reason, those reasons so rarely end up being made clear.

No matter the type of men you've been with, chased after, or settled down with, one thing is certain: these experiences will lead you where you need to be. You need to take these lessons, the good and bad, and make something of yourself. The day I swore off love, and finally decided to focus on my well-being, was the day that changed my life forever. It was after a long week of partying with Dee and Margarita, and I was feeling like I needed a deep cleanse. I was in the shower, washing away sweat, liquor and disgrace. My life had taken a turn and not in the direction that I wanted it to go. When I was growing up, my mom was very forceful when it came to education. My family in general was big on me becoming a strong, independent woman. They all admired me for my feminine figure and manly ways. On the outside I seemed to be well put together, but what people didn't know was the internal struggle I was fighting. Most of which resulted from the lengthy dating history I had accumulated. I was always the girl that envisioned myself getting married, being in a relationship, who was almost codependent when dating. I didn't have daddy issues. I had an amazing childhood. I got whatever I wanted, went wherever I wanted, and did whatever I wanted. It was the ideal situation for a young girl trying to mature into something bigger. Along the way, my heart had been torn, ripped out, sewed back together, and then frozen. I froze out all feelings from my being. I refused to accept love from wherever it was trying to find me. I couldn't even have a normal conversation without feeling like something was wrong, something was missing. So, there I was, in the shower, talking to the universe. I usually do my talking to the universe in the shower, or in my car. I tried to put out good, positive vibes and pray that positivity would radiate upon me like the Florida heat. I let the water drain away my tears, I opened my eyes and smiled. I vowed to myself I would no longer search for love. I will search for self-perseverance, motivation and hope. Despite all the feelings and traits I had lost along the way, I never gave up hope. I'm an optimist in many forms.

Getting out of the shower, I wrapped myself in a towel and stared in the mirror. Despite the negative feelings I was having, I continued to repeat that I will no longer seek a man. My life does not have to be determined by whether or not I'm in a relationship. I needed to focus on myself, love myself again. That same teacher that told me Nelly and I were like oil and water also told me to never change myself for a man, and to always be Cindy. I had changed, when I looked at myself, after all of this newfound knowledge, I realized that I was no longer the Cindy I knew. I knew that some change was good, learning from your mistakes was good, but I was losing track of my goals and self-worth. I didn't like that idea. I was scared that I could never get my old self back. If I could go back and comfort that hungover self, I wouldn't. If I would have comforted her, she wouldn't have gotten the wakeup call she so sorely needed, and she never would have gained that self-respect back.

It turns out that when you love yourself, good things happen. I had become Senior Class President, Deputy Brigade Commander in charge of 13 high schools in my county, and was working two jobs, an assistant at a law firm and a hostess at Olive Garden. I was too busy to focus on men. I needed a break. Instead, I was fixing myself. I had become stronger. My will to survive in this barbaric world expanded and I felt deeper than ever. I became fierce. This positivity led to an unexpected trip to New York City for the summer, versus my annual Euro trip that usually led to war stories.

I spent the entire summer with my girl crew, six of us total, crammed in a two-bedroom apartment, with nothing but fun in the sun during the day and the bright city lights at night. My personal brand was growing, my mind was eager, and overall, my inner self was developing. That summer, I had the sexiest sun-kissed tan, with matching caramel highlights, and my weight had returned to a normal coke bottle image. I was taking the steamiest selfies for social media and gaining more followers than I knew what to do with. For the first time in a long time I didn't need a man to do it for me, I was loving myself.

SUMMARY

Being a positive person takes effort and time. You must be patient and kind to see the good in all the evil. To stay strong, one must simply keep an open mind and an open heart. Even the deepest wounds can be healed with love. To any woman scorned, you need to know it's not the end of the world. Although it may feel that way, there is more out there. You need to remember the grass isn't greener on the other side, grass only gets greener if you keep watering it. Love is a complicated game that rarely ends with a defined winner and loser. Most of the time, women feel like they are losing the game.

That summer that I looked better than ever ended up being the summer I met The One. I have heard that once you stop looking for love it will find you. That was something I had thought about that day in the shower when I swore off love and swore on a lifetime of self-fulfillment. I said to myself, imagine I find love after finally accepting the fact that I don't need it, or want it for that matter. Life is funny, but it's also a bitch. In my case, that's exactly what happened. The minute I found myself indulging in my own brilliance was the same minute the future love of my life walked down those four concrete steps, making eye contact with me and changing my life forever. The moral of loving yourself is simple. If you don't love yourself, who will? Your parents might tell you you're special, but unless you do something of importance for yourself, then they're just lying to you. Don't make whoever it is that says you're special a liar. Be true to yourself. Learn to love you. The good, the bad, the ugly, the ashamed and hungover. You all deserve to love, if not someone else, then yourself. Life is too short to self-hate, or to shame yourself. Every woman is beautiful. We are all made different for a reason, because if we all looked plastic like a famous fake family on TV we all know, well, then the world wouldn't be interesting. Write your own story, follow your heart, and let the men chase you, because darling, you're worth the chase.

THE ONE

Life is not a fairytale, unfortunately. We can't all be princesses and not every man is Prince Charming. We can, however, make our own realistic love story that is raw, true and you. The last breed of a man, and the rarest, will be referred to as The One. The One is right for you, not anyone else. I truly believe in soulmates, and that every person has another individual to complete them. After all, we have two eyes, ears, arms, legs, but only one heart. Your soulmate should be the one who completes the set to your heart. Two hearts entwined together like vines. Usually whenever you come across The One, it is clear that there is a connection unlike any you've had before. He will not play games, like The Character or The Bad Boy. Instead, he will have a Prince Charming vibe, for real. He has a respectful brand, close with his family, reliable to his friends. The One won't have a novel-long history of partners, and he will have his shit together. He may not be a millionaire living in a mansion with a retirement plan and cars to spare, but when it comes to a man's comfort levels, such as home, job, and car, he will have it together. No man that isn't established in those three areas will ever be ready to settle down. Make sure the man has an established home, whether with his family or on his own. Bouncing back and forth or living month to month in different apartments every other month, is not established. His job life must be secure too. He needs to love his job or at least have an interest in what he does. The same goes for a man and his car. If your man doesn't have a reliable form of transportation, chances are his mental state is just as scattered. Just like women need to learn to love themselves, men have work to do before they can settle down. Instead of your typical encounters with the other types of men, a special bond is made within seconds of meeting The One. There's a vibe to him that you've never encountered before. Decades later, you will still be able to remember the outfit he was wearing the first time you met. You will remember glances he gave you, and you will remember sensations running through you that feel like they're on fire. You will just remember it being different. Different is good. Change is good, and The One is exactly that: The One.

My first encounter with The One occurred completely by accident. My cousin Samantha was engaged to a man named Andy. This was the summer I had finally learned to love myself, and my crew of six was throwing a backyard BBQ party. Samantha naturally invited Andy, who decided he would bring a cousin and a friend. The entire time I was preparing drinks and pacing myself, because I learned from past experiences just how sick I could get. The other girls were discussing who was coming and whether or not they were hot. Samantha was letting them know that Andy's cousin was single, cute, but into Spanish girls so, being Eastern European, our crew didn't have a chance. I chose to stray away from the conversation only because my past self would have pounced on whoever came through the door in order to claim dominance of the situation. I was desperate for love back then and I decided right then and there that if I was going to keep things different, I would be different. I not only avoided the greeting of the guests, but the actual arrival of them, too. While the girls lined up at the stairway to welcome the guests, I had already snuck out, trying to make it to the backyard with my drink, planning on lighting a cigarette to ease the stress of the situation. I love my girls, but it was just a weird situation. They were already talking about the single man who was scheduled to attend, fighting over who would have him. I turned the corner to the backyard, lit my cigarette, and held my drink in the other hand.

I was posted up against the wall, into my mood and the background music, when I heard footsteps down the hallway heading for my direction. By the time I looked up, I only saw one person. He was tall, fairly built, and clad in dark blue jeans, white T-shirt, and fresh white Jordans. My jaw most likely dropped to the floor because I could barely hear Andy behind him saying hey, pointing the guys in the direction of Samantha and the others. I slowly smirked and went back to my business, but I saw him glancing at me from the corner of his eye. Bond, what I will be calling him, was the shy type, was sitting by himself most of the night, an observer. Whenever I'd pass by, I could feel him glancing, but he never said a word. I'd smile at him, naturally, it was hard not to. He would smile back, then quickly look away. This led me to believe he wasn't interested, but I couldn't get over the fact that I felt something. Something I never felt before. I could sense an actual sweetness to this man, and not like that of The Sweetheart. He was sincere, and kind, and when one of the girls asked him where the best clubs were, insinuating that they go together, he responded by saying he's not much for the clubs but that he'd be happy to tell her the hot spots he knew of. A man like The Character, or the Bad Boy would have been on that like white on rice, talking about let's go right now, I'll show you. Instead, he had class. He was clean cut and had an innocence about him that, no matter how much detail I go into, it wouldn't do him justice. He was a real-life Prince Charming. I couldn't believe that he was standing only inches away. It was surreal, but I kept my cool and my pants buttoned. I barely said two words to the guy. He eventually left because two of the girls were fighting for his attention, even though those same girls deny it. To this day they won't admit it was over him, but I was there, it was over him. He became so uncomfortable over the girls' bickering, he ended up leaving. He didn't say goodbye, he didn't look back, and to be honest, I didn't even see him leave. I came back from the backyard waiting to see him sitting on the corner of the couch he had been in for almost three hours, and nothing. I felt empty. A man I didn't even know or talk to had left such an impact on me. I couldn't stop thinking about him (it was kind of hard when the two girls kept screaming over him). I'm sure the whole building couldn't stop thinking about him, how loud they were. As quick and abruptly as he came into my life, he was gone just as fast.

My summer ended without me seeing him again. I wasn't exaggerating when I said he's an innocent type of man. The weeks passed, and it was time for me to return home. I returned to my everyday routine between school and work, and almost forgot that I had ever met him. It wasn't until I got a new message notification on Facebook that I remembered how I felt when I first saw him. Opening it, I realized it was from Bond. He wrote simply, with class, and in Bosnian-Croatian, our native language, "Hey, you are beyond beautiful."

I melted. Literally, my entire body felt like mush, from the neck down I felt like I had melted into a puddle. I put my phone away without responding and I'm not going to lie, I forgot to respond. How could I forget to respond to such a fairytale perfect man? Easy. Life. I had focused my life so hard in a direction I needed it to go. At the time, I was leaving work, which led to a night-long study session, which repeated in the morning. With all seriousness, as melted as I was, I didn't know what to say. The old me would have started with the games, the flirtation and the same old nonsense that made me hate myself to begin with. I decided to leave it in my inbox. Then, it was time for my Christmas trip to New York City.

I landed in New York and decided the first thing I would do, before breathing, would be to respond to his message. I said thank you and let him know that I was back in his neighborhood if he ever wanted to meet. I put my phone away, took a breath of garbage smelling air, because that's what it smells like outside of JFK airport, and continued my journey. That winter break, we saw a lot of each other, mostly because Samantha and Andy were hot and heavy for each other. We all lived for the night life and would make it a group event every weekend. Hookah lounges, McDonalds, regular bars, the beach, you name it, we were there. Each time we met up, Bond and I would get a few words out of each other. After about three nights out, we were at a Hookah lounge when everyone disappeared from the draped off V.I.P. room, everyone but Bond and me. He sat across from me, typing away on his BlackBerry, or pretending to. I sat, legs crossed, hands crossed, head slightly tilted with a smile on my face, just staring at him, enjoying the view (or looking creepy). I don't know how but I found the courage to stand and join him on the other side of the table. I looked down at his phone, realizing he wasn't doing anything important. Much like my prediction, he was faking it. I leaned in and asked if he was ever going to talk to me directly, one on one. He barely looked up, face red as blood, then smirked and said yeah. I then took his BlackBerry from his hands, my fingers slightly gliding across his, and began putting in my BBM pin. Back in the day, BlackBerry Messenger was life and giving away your pin was safer than giving a man your number. I handed him the phone, smiled, and over the music I loudly said,

"There you go; you don't have to talk to me if you're shy, but you can text me."

Without waiting for a response, I confidently stood and returned to my side of the table. By the time I sat down, my BlackBerry had received a request from the one and only Bond.

Now this may all seem so elementary, which it is, but it's a breath of fresh air when you compare The One with my encounters with those of different types. In my case, Bond was very shy. Most men considered The One are of the shyer variety and take time to open up. With this breed of men, adventure comes with experience. The more experiences you share, the more adventure is going to show up. Bond was a man who had his three categories set in stone and established. His living situation, although with his parents and brother, was established. Along with his professional career and his brand-new Audi A-4. All of his boxes had been checked off, and now mine was next.

When it came to The One, we took things slow and became friends. Good friends, for that matter. We shared emotions, and our innermost feelings and secrets. This was something rare to come by. If a man is at all interested in what's going on in your brain, more often than not, he will fall under The One category. With all the other men, it was a constant chase, chasing him and chasing what he was feeling or thinking. With The One, it comes naturally whether you want it to or not. It just happens. It feels right. This slow, steady pace is a recipe for success. Getting to know the other person internally, and not over a sexual encounter, is empowering. Sharing more than just your bodies is hard to do with the other four types of men, but not so much with The One. He has a purity about him that is easy and admirable, it draws you in for the long haul rather than the addictive nature of the Bad Boy.

Within a couple of weeks, we were texting good mornings and good nights. I would hide in my friends closet to talk for hours with him, hoping Samantha wouldn't find out. She wasn't too delighted that her first cousin was building an emotional connection with her soon-to-be in-law. This was a force that no one could stop, not even us. It's a magical experience, much like a real-life fairytale. A sense of security comes with this type of man. That's the biggest quality that comes with him, feeling secure and safe. I never felt safe with the other types, I was always anxious and waiting for the other shoe to drop. The One will ease your mind, he will not give you any reason to question or doubt him. You will know when you meet The One because there are emotions that come with him that you have never experienced and will never experience with anyone else. He will be your real-life Prince Charming, and he will make you feel like a princess. If not a princess, then a queen. Our souls connected, our minds were in sync, our desires were the same, and conversation came easy. There isn't anything in the world you would change about him, and there isn't anything that he would change about you. It is a pure love, built from an innocent friendship. A connection that can never and will never be broken.

That was the most romantic Christmas vacation I'd ever had. I spent most of it with Bond under the bright city lights. As if the city weren't bright already, imagine it during the most wonderful time of the year. Corny Christmas music filled the streets, trees lit up on every corner, and not a star in sight but you know they're there. You can feel them, the alignment of the stars, the sun and the moon, everything is just perfect when you're together. When you encounter the man who will be your one and only, try not to have sex on the first date. More than likely, he won't be The One if you have sex on the first night. This kind of man won't allow it, it's a respect thing. You want to be intuitionally in sync before you sync your bodies. Trust me, it makes the sex so much better. Once you're mentally and emotionally connected to someone, your souls coming together as one, the natural force of a physical relationship will literally be like a volcanic eruption.

Our last night, the group went out in one of the biggest snowstorms New York City had ever seen. Of course, we didn't get the weather update that said we should stay indoors. Instead, we were lounge-bound for a great night out. We enjoyed great music and good drinks. We finished it off with a huge snowball fight in the middle of the street. Before I knew it, I was on a flight back home, reminiscing on everything that had happened the past three weeks.

Then it was time to go back to reality. I had to leave my real-life fairytale and my real-life Prince Charming. It was like waking up from a dream and finding out that none of it ever happened. I couldn't fathom that I had met a man, hung out with him months later, and now, with no physical way of seeing him, those electrifying feelings were starting to fade. With your everyday life comes a dose of reality. I could no longer see him whenever I wanted, and I had school and two jobs to keep up with. Yet again, I lost everyday contact with Bond and after a month or so, things went back to normal. I was back to focusing on myself, to the stability of self-love. Being able to love yourself and focus on yourself for a long while is important. You don't want to lose sight of your goals, and most importantly you do not want to fall back into old habits. Even though I had pushed Bond into the farthest part of my brain, I refused to reconnect with old flames or make new ones. Once a woman encounters her one and only, this becomes easy. All other men fade away and it seems impossible to be with anyone else You don't want to screw up a good thing, you want to focus on making it better. This is the path I decided to take.

Looking back, I know that The One had wished I stayed in better contact with him whenever I would go back to reality, but I had been through a lot of hard break ups and I still needed time to focus on loving myself. No woman should lose herself over a man, even if he is The One. The moment you lose focus of yourself and your goals is the moment you could lose the man who should be your forever. If a man is falling for you, he's falling for you because of the way you are, not who you were or are going to be. If you change, so will the relationship. If you are both growing in your own ways, and headed in the same direction, you're golden. Sometimes individuals can grow in opposite directions, that can happen, but if it does that will more than likely lead to the realization that he was never The One and was probably more of The Sweetheart type. The One is connected to you, and you are connected to him. No matter the distance or the craziness of your everyday life, you both will be in sync. Much like Bond and myself, even if you lose contact for a short amount of time, that doesn't mean you should go and physically connect with other people. You both work toward a common goal of wanting to be together in the long run. Rome wasn't built in a day, right? Well, neither was any long-lasting relationship. Things of beauty take time and patience. As women, we want things when we want them and how we want them. During my self-love process, patience was my main focus. Unfortunately, you can't force time, I tried.

Bond and I had our first real date one year later. It was Christmas time again in New York City and it was just as beautiful as ever. Our first date was not extravagant. It's not where you go, it's who you're with. He picked me up, on foot, and we walked to a local Dunkin' Donuts. My first date ever with The One and only of my life, was at a donut shop. My kind of man. We sat down and talked for close to three hours. He wanted to take me to a movie, but I refused. My cousin was calling me, they needed their champion back for a round of Ring of Fire, and as bad as it sounds, I skipped out on the movie with Bond to go back to my crew. It wasn't that I was having a bad time, or that I didn't want to go, I just knew myself way too well. If I was alone with this fine specimen of a man in a dark movie theater, it would be a recipe for disaster. Been there, done that. I needed to stray from my usual ways, so instead, I insisted he walk me home and save the movie for a part two date. Instead of being upset, like most types of men would be (we know they love to have it their way), he smiled and agreed. He pulled my chair out for me, held the door, and then held his hand out for mine. The moment we interlocked hands was the moment I knew that I never wanted to hold another man's hand ever again. Our hands fit perfectly, like puzzle pieces. He gave the back of my hand a slight caress, as if he were comforting me. It worked, I felt very comfortable and felt a lot of other things for that matter. We had started our long walk back to my cousin's apartment when it began raining. Bond pulled an umbrella out from behind him, like a magic trick. I hadn't even noticed the umbrella the entire time we were together. Romantically, he held it out and leaned it more on my side so I wouldn't get wet. This was the first time in my entire life a man was catering to my needs. He actually cared if I got sick or not and was adamant that he didn't mind getting sick as long as I was okay. This breed of man is rare, and when you find him, ladies, embrace it. Be loved, be treated right, and let him take care of you. Every now and then it's nice to be taken care of.

As we slowly approached my cousin's apartment building, we stood face to face for about five minutes. Not saying a word, just appreciating and examining each other's facial expressions. I fell in love with his hazel eyes, the beauty mark on his cheek, and his slightly crooked smile. I felt so lucky to be with him. Toward the end of our first official date, he slowly closed the umbrella. Even though we were starting to get soaking wet, we kept staring at each other, smiling. Waiting. Before I knew it, I could see him coming in slowly, carefully, as if trying to read my reaction. Such a gentleman. I willingly and excitedly began falling forward into him. We had the sweetest, most romantic kiss in the rain, even *The Notebook* couldn't compare. Okay, I'm lying, but we were definitely a close second. I could feel his hand around the small of my back, and I found my hands wrapped around him. The rain was dripping down our faces, by this time we were both soaked and in love. We stood there, his hand on my waist, my hands on his face. He flashed me his beautiful, slightly crooked smile, and I flashed one back. I leaned in again, kissing him first this time, and he responded. We unlatched and before I knew it, our first date had come to an end.

Over a year later, and after losing contact again, I was heading on a business trip to Canada. In a wild coincidence, Bond contacted me asking when I would be visiting New York again. Lucky for him, at the end of my Canada trip I would be staying the night in New York before returning back to Florida. He wanted to make a date out of it, and we did. I was traveling with a friend of Dee's and Margarita's, and when we finished our business and got to New York, we realized they only had one room with a king size bed. We took it because that was the best hotel with a bar, and I figured I might be able to make other arrangements if all went well. I invited Bond to join us at the hotel bar, and he decided to show up with Andy and another friend. By this point, Andy and Samantha had broken up, never married. I had not seen him since he was with my cousin, and I hadn't seen Bond in quite a while either. Before they arrived, I ran into the waitress in the bathroom. I briefly told her my situation, and explained she needed to keep the drinks coming.

"Oh, damn! Girl, I got you!" she exclaimed.

She lived up to my expectation because I was feeling nice by the time they arrived, and I had the courage to enjoy myself and our evening.

Halfway through the dinner, and however many shots later, I leaned into Bond and whispered, "We only have one bed in our hotel room, I'm not really comfortable with that. I'd rather stay at your place for the night, if that's okay?"

He rubbed the outside of my thigh, grabbed my hand, leaned in and said, "Of course."

With those two words, I knew our relationship was about to take a crazy turn. Turns out my womanly sixth sense was right. We decided to call it a night, I told my business partner I'd be back in the morning in time for our flight. He agreed, and Bond and I headed for the door. Andy and his friend following behind us. We said quick good-byes to everyone, and the next thing I knew, we were in front of Bond's apartment building.

"Will your parents be awake?" I asked, realizing I'd forgotten to address this earlier.

"No," he lied.

We walked up two flights of stairs, turned left, and he put the key in the door, but before he could unlock it, I stopped him.

"Seriously, make sure your parents are asleep because I can't meet them like this. It's wildly inappropriate," I said nervously.

He unlocked and opened the door, then turned and whispered, "Wait here."

Within seconds, he waved someone out of the room and then turned to give me the all clear. Turns out my future father in-law had been watching movies on his laptop and was kicked out of the living room because his son was bringing home a girl. It honestly didn't look like the first time Bond had in shooing his father away, but I try not to focus on those negative details.

We spent the night watching a Zac Efron movie, cuddled on his bed. It started off innocent and led to a typical make-out session. Which then led to Netflix and chill. A few minutes in, I stopped. I told him I couldn't do it, that I didn't want to start a relationship by having a sexual encounter on the first night. I got scared that I broke my number one rule with The One in sleeping with him on our first date (okay not really our first date, but our first date in over a year). I didn't want him to hit it and quit it. I was terrified that I was repeating what happened with The Character, Al, and that the minute I left for Florida I would never hear from him again. Apparently, even if you have sex the first sleepover you have with The One, it isn't a one-and-done.

SUMMARY

Thirteen years after laying eyes on Bond at a summer BBQ party, and nine years of being together, we were engaged for eight years, and now have been happily married for one month with two children. Even though he is The One, we had to go through a lot of bullshit, a lot of tears, arguments, and almost two real breakups, and we came out stronger than ever. He still treats me with the same respect as he did on day one. He still holds my chair out for me and opens the door for me, the whole works. Our souls are still on the same path. No relationship is perfect, but if you find The One and you're able to work together and most of all, communicate, you are set for a successful future.

EVERYONE NEEDS A FRIEND

No matter what stage of life you're in, you will always need a friend. Single, dating, married, divorcing, you need someone to confide in. Having someone there to balance the insecurities in your mind and the whirlwind of emotions that overcome us in the dating world is important. You need a safe haven. Otherwise, the damage could be detrimental. You don't want to end up having a mental breakdown when you're sitting in the middle of traffic at a red light, see a guy who hit it and quit it, and the next thing you know your car is in park and you're banging on the hood of his car, asking why he never called you back. Don't be that girl – and yes, I actually saw that happen. A full-grown woman, divorced with a pre-teen daughter, fully lost her shit in 5 o'clock traffic. If she were my friend, I wouldn't let a bitch end up on the evening news, classified as a "Road Rager".

Get yourself a squad, and whenever you end a relationship or a fling, call those men out. Let your feelings and emotions out, give the man a funny nickname and turn those heartbreaks into heartfelt moments with your girls. The friends you surround yourself with are the people who are there for you. They will listen, no matter how many times you complain about the same type of man. No matter how annoying you get, I'm positive one of them will put you in check. I know that Dee and Margarita are those friends for me. We sit, laughing about past flings, and call them out even years later. It is a form of therapy, without the price tag. If you're a secretive person, or just don't like sharing your emotions, then write it down. Burn it at the next bonfire. Do whatever it takes to call out the man that wasn't for you and move on. You do not want to miss your Prince Charming because you're infatuated with what could have been. Many women have made that mistake, and all of them regret it.

If dating isn't your thing, or you don't want it to be your thing any longer, change your status. Get yourself an entourage you can travel, explore and make memories with. Having a good group of friends, or even just one friend, can make all the difference for your future love life. You should also remember that the pack you travel with is a resemblance of who you are or who you want to be, so choose wisely. Much like dating, you could find yourself surrounded by the wrong friends. It's not a permanent decision that the friends you choose reflect who you are, but on the outside looking in, it can cause a reflection which could potentially draw the wrong audience.

Having the right support system makes all the difference when it comes to dating and finding love. You need friends or family to put you in check when you start to become a little unrealistic, or even if you end up acting out of character. You need them for when things go bad, and you especially want them around when things go right. Having people to celebrate with is important for anyone to be happy. When something great happens, who do you notify? Probably your support system. And the same thing goes for when things don't work out.

SUMMARY

Friendships are just like romantic relationships. They take time, they take work, and they take compromise. They not only need to be there for you, but you need to be there for them. If you know you're not giving it your all, your friends will feel that energy.

Being able to have these good friends can define how you interact with a man. If you're able to have a few good close friends that you're open with and can full heartedly love, chances are you'll be able to do the same thing once you've found a man. If you're unable to open up and communicate with your friends, how can you expect yourself to be open with a man? Take a look at your entourage and ask yourself if they're your support system. Through the good and bad, sickness and health, are these people there for you always? If so, I'm sure we can all agree that it's a great feeling.

THERAPY IS FOR EVERYONE

I was pregnant with my second child when my husband and I almost broke up. We'd finally had enough. We both felt that we had given the relationship, and each other, all of our time, love and energy. Calling it quits felt like the last option. But we agreed that we were going to try everything before we officially called it. The last tactic we could think of was going to couples' counseling. We agreed that we wouldn't sugarcoat things, we would lay it all out on the table and if the other person got mad, so be it. We were all in. Whatever was meant to be would be.

Through therapy, we learned that we were speaking different languages. Different love languages. But with therapy, we learned how to speak to each other. We learned how to love each other the way we should have been loving each other all this time. There were concerns that he had that I had no idea were even an issue, and vice versa.

We're not the type of people to air our laundry for the world to see, but we knew that if we wanted a life together, we needed to let it all out there and try to make things work. After a few sessions, and doing our homework, we fell more in love with each other than the day we met. We were able to appreciate the sacrifices, the time, the energy, the EVERYTHING that goes into a relationship, and we saw that the other person meant well. We still loved each other, more than ever. We wanted to communicate, and to hear each other, actually *hear* each other. One of the rarest things you'll find in a relationship is open communication, where the other individual actually listens to what you're saying. Our therapist, Dr. P., was astonished at our progress and how hard we were both working toward our relationship. She said that she's never met a couple who was as motivated and successful as we were. We put in the work, did our homework, went on date nights, stopped making everything about the kids, and started talking each other's languages. It felt impossible at first, but with every conversation and with every encounter, it became easier and more natural.

To this day, we have coffee every afternoon. No interruptions, no kids, no phones, no outsiders, just us and our coffee. We take turns talking about our days, about our worries, our excitements. We support each other and constantly ask "What do you think?" before we move onto the next conversation. I felt close to Bond before, but after these exercises became our normal everyday talk, I feel like we're more fused than ever before. We have an unbreakable bond that you only see in Hallmark movies. If a Hallmark movie had couples therapy in it.

Neither of us were fans of therapy before this. We didn't think it would work, but that's not how we went into it. We went into it thinking that this would be the thing to change our perspectives and our relationship. We knew that if this didn't work, we would have to explain to our two little boys that Mommy and Daddy fell out of love and were better as friends.

Because of therapy, and our willingness to work together, we are still together. We are stronger than ever. We continue to communicate in each other's languages. We continue to go for "checkups" with Dr. P., and she continues to be amazed at how far we've come, even in a short amount of time. From bi-weekly sessions to once a year, we make the most of every meeting with her. We continue to work on our marriage.

Because for better or worse, therapy is for everyone. Don't knock it till you try it.

SUMMARY

If you're in a relationship and you haven't gone to couples' therapy, you need to. If you have yet to find someone, keep in mind that when you do, you'll want to go to couples' therapy. Even if nothing is wrong, and everything feels right, do yourself a favor and go to at least one session. See how you feel afterward. If anything, think of it as a third party looking into your relationship, and telling you point blank what's working and what's not. It will only benefit you. You don't want to waste 10 years only to figure out that the person you're with isn't your person. A lot of pain and passion can be created and healed with therapy, you just have to give it a chance.

THE POINT

The point of this book is to show you that relationships are a never-ending work in progress. The relationship we have with ourselves is most important, and love will come and go out of your life. Whether that means friends, boyfriends, husbands, whatever. Learning to love yourself will bring great joy, and great sex, into your life. Know yourself, your mind, your body, and the type of man you want to spend forever with – or at least the next decade or so.

I recently spoke with a married woman, her second marriage, and she told me that in life and love you can either have fun in your marriage or have peace in your marriage, but you cannot have both. She said she would rather have fun and cry every once in a while, than have peace and be bored. She compared herself and her marriage to those of her friends and explained that no marriage or relationship is the same. This woman is now divorced for a second time. Some women handle it all: the breadwinners who take care of the kids and handle the home and everything that comes with it. Some women share those responsibilities with their husband or boyfriend. And some women don't handle any of it, their significant other does. I couldn't get this idea out of my head - fun or peace. It made me reflect on my own marriage, my own situation, relationships as a whole, and there is some truth in it.

This bit of advice deeply troubled me. I began to think back on all my relationships, to search for the answer within them. If I had gone and married a type of man such as The Character or The Bad Boy, I would be having a lot of fun. It would be a fantastic time most days, but I know deep down that it would not be peaceful. But then I thought of Bond and I's relationship. Do we not have fun? Why can't a woman be at peace and find the fun? If you're in a peaceful relationship but find yourself struggling to have fun, why can't we as women use our powers to create a more fun environment? I find myself in a stable relationship, one that I find to be completely satisfying and in those moments of boredom, I find the fun and bring it to the relationship.

Relationships are a choice. From the moment you wake up, you have a choice as to whether or not you want to keep going. Keep trying. Keep pushing. If you're with the right person, these choices aren't usually hard to make. Sometimes they are, sure. No one's fuckin' perfect. If you find yourself constantly fighting with negative thoughts and feelings about your current relationship, then something is wrong. Extremely wrong.

Being able to have an out of body experience is almost necessary for relationships to work. You need to be able to see your situation for what it is, or at least attempt to. If you know that there is something wrong, but you want to fix it, then do something about it. Couples therapy? Maybe just therapy for you? Maybe you're unhappy with something that your significant other doesn't have control over? Whatever the problem is, put your big girl panties on and figure your shit out. No one is going to figure it out for you.

SUMMARY

You want a man? Go to reasonable locations to find one! You have a man but he's not satisfying you? Either fix it or get a new man! There is no one-and-done solution to anyone's problems. The best we can do is apply a process of elimination. Start with one solution, give it X amount of time, and if it works – TA-DAAA, you're happy. Call me your fairy godmother. If it doesn't work, Google a counselor, therapist, or a goddamn priest if you have to.

The answers to all your problems are right in front of your face. Cliché? I know. But it's true! The type of energy you put out into the Universe is the type of energy you will get back. Are you the type of bad bitch that can't find a man worth a damn? Get over yourself, dig deep, and really figure out what your issue is with men. There is a world full of possibilities, and I refuse to accept the idea that there is not one person made for you out there. THERE IS! He, or she, is out there! You just need to be at peace with yourself, love yourself, and send whatever vibes you want to attract into the world.

LIFE IS HARD, LOVE IS HARDER

Calling out a man is releasing. I have called out multiple men, in the form of five categories: 1. The Character, 2. The Sweetheart, 3. The Mistake, 4. The Bad Boy and 5. The One. You can settle down with any one of the five types. There are different types of women who all have different romantic needs. Each of these different types of women will need to be called out at some point as well. It's a two-way street. Whether it be the woman who chose the wrong type of a man, or vice versa. I found that characterizing the men into these five groups narrows it down for easiest understanding. I grew up with two brothers, one I classify as The Bad Boy and the other, The Character. I have a country full of male cousins that all vary among the five groups, and I love each one of them. I wouldn't have Dee or Margarita try to marry any of them, though. I know better. If you're trying to find your one and only, take your time because if you're looking in the wrong places, the right man could pass you by. Most importantly, you need to learn to love yourself. I'm not referring to a self-obsession, but rather, a genuine love and respect that you give yourself each day. As this book comes to an end I have some takeaways I don't want you to forget.

Life is hard, love is harder. There are no cheat sheets, or unknown secrets that can help ease the process. What does help is knowing the types of love you can have with different types of men. Not every man is the same; they don't love the same or disrespect the same. Much like snowflakes, each one has his own unique pattern to separate them from the rest. Just like no woman is the same. If you're not looking for love, then embrace yourself. Look for love in your own heart. Do not let any type of man change who you're destined to be. Don't let them win, and don't respond to old flames years later. It's a dangerous game that you're likely to lose. No one wins in those instances. Marriages, hearts and sometimes even faces get broken.

It's not all about men, it's about YOU. Throughout this life of love, I've realized that it's not all about the men. It's also about self-awareness and self-worth. Like I've stated previously, the energy you put out into the world is the energy that will return to you. You want to make sure you're established as a woman. Just like men need the three things to feel self-sufficient, which we briefly discussed when talking about Bond, women need to do the same. Do not live life thinking you need a man to make your life complete. You make your life complete. You were born by yourself, and you will die by yourself. Unless you're like Noah and Allie from The Notebook. There are stories like that, but again, being established in your own ways is the only thing you need to succeed and to accomplish a life of love. Make sure you have your own taken care of. Get an education, see the world, make friends and long-lasting memories. For the women who feel they have to be in a relationship, go for it, but don't give all of your heart to one man right away. You will just find yourself broken and alone after it's all said and done. Instead, enjoy the company and make memories. Learn lessons and grow from each situation or relationship. Use your newfound knowledge to better your life, to further it. Become someone, make a difference and be happy.

BE PATIENT! Women rush into these things for lots of reasons, the most common being that their biological clock is ticking. Stop with that. Technology has advanced and if it's really for that reason, you have options. Freeze your eggs and there you go; your clock is no longer ticking. Now you will have all the time in the world to find someone. There could be a good reason you haven't found The One yet, maybe you think you're established but you're really not. That's not a bad thing, it just means that your life isn't where it should be yet, and you need to give it time. Being patient is god's greatest gift. Or whoever's gift it is I'm not sure, but you need to learn how to be patient with love, with your future husband, and most definitely with yourself. If you can truly master the ancient virtue of patience, you're set for life. Time will ensure that you find your special someone, patience helps you get there.

Dating should be fun, not a job. You get to meet new people from all over, who do different things for a living. You get to go places you might normally not go to and you build experience and memories all in one. If you find that dating is not a fun game for you, don't do it, because it's not an automatic that you will meet The One on a blind date your friends set you up on or through a dating site. Some women love the journey of finding true love, and others aren't cut out for it. I enjoyed the journey while I was on it but wished I didn't travel so many miles before finding it. Yet looking back, I wouldn't change anything because that could mean changing my current situation and I would never change my life. The goal of this shout out list is to provide the necessary information and real-life stories to help guide you on a path that you will eventually love. You won't want to go back in time and undo a date or forget that you met some type of man. I'm warning you now who you should stay far from.

Try new things. I've been through the struggles of life and continue to face more. Overall, I've become accustomed to the rollercoaster it can be. It's a vicious cycle for women, much like the menstrual cycle we deal with. You go through the phases of looking good, feeling good, and then downfall into bloating depression and so on and so forth. Whenever you are feeling down and negative, the longer you stay there, the worse it will get. Put your big girl panties on and push through it. Cry it, sing it, dance it, eat it, binge watch it away. If you're constantly battling yourself, you will never find The One. You have to look good, feel good, and do good. No man wants a hot mess, they want a successful, open-minded woman. Never say never and try new things. Be a better you. What a cliché, I know. But, it's true. You don't want a man that is stuck in his ways or that is not open to trying what you like, so why follow that trend? Bond and I constantly discuss our passions and what would make us happy, and the other person has to suck it up and go along. If I didn't force him to become a romantic, we never would have lasted. For a man who grew up in a house where hugs were nonexistent, love was shown through providing versus cuddling. Whereas, in my home, all we did was cuddle and give kisses and say I love you to one another. Molding our love languages to complement the other's is not something every person can do. That means you cannot find love in someone that is incapable of molding. If he is the way he is, well, honey, there's plenty of other men out there. If you're with a man that is strictly a physical lover, and you're a known prude, well you won't get anywhere in that relationship. If he's a stay-at-home nerd and you're borderline Marilyn Monroe, well, that won't work either. Connecting and communicating is a great basis for a foundation with a man. No matter his type, if you can connect and communicate, there's hope.

Communication is key. There have been times I wanted to call it quits with Bond, and vice versa. That is a real relationship. Anyone who says otherwise is lying, especially if you have small kids. Adulting is hard, relationships are hard, and parenting is harder. Mix the three together and you're destined for disasters. However, if you have a stable connection and open communication, you will get through it. Any man not willing to connect or communicate is simply not interested. He is not interested in the longevity of the relationship nor the seriousness of it. You can spend a decade on a man with no such luck, he can turn around, leave, find another lover and magically he's an open book. It's not your fault, the only thing that is your fault was staying so damn long. Sometimes you are both willing to connect and communicate, but you are just wrong for each other.

Learn how to speak your partner's language! I strongly believe in the love languages and if you're able to get your significant other to take that test, do it. It's very important to understand each other in a way that you might not have prior to your relationship. Use your resources. If you're not a romantic, Google ways to romance your significant other. If you don't know how to cook and your man is dying for a meal, Google easy recipes. It's a commitment, it's a two-way street. Women, if you are constantly trying to satisfy your man and he just isn't having it. Stop. Be your own person. Make yourself happy. If he's The One for you, he will come around and fix himself, if he isn't, then let him go. You're holding onto someone else's forever. There were so many men I've met and could have made a future with, but they weren't for me. The split second I realized that they were not my cup of tea, I let them go – no questions asked. They simply belonged to another woman. Whether they knew it then or not, it's true. Every person has a soul mate. Whether it's a man or a best friend, there is one person in the world out there for you that simply connects to you. Ying to your yang, salt to your pepper, whatever the analogy, it's true. A happy relationship is the hardest thing you could work on, and sorry to say, it is a never-ending job.

Establish yourself first, then find love. I've been through every phase a woman can go through in a relationship, the exciting, the desperate, the casual sex, the long-lasting, the infatuation, the regret. You name it and I've been there. All of these led to a common result, a disastrous end to a potential forever love. Each man I met made me stronger, eventually. That doesn't mean you want to go out there having sex with anyone who walks by or giving your heart and soul to anyone in the name of making yourself stronger. You need to keep your cool. Establish yourself, have fun with your friends, make memories, live for yourself. Coincidences can happen. I was sure that some men were meant to be mine. They weren't. I was not established enough as a woman for it to work out. If you find a man you're just in complete awe of, observe his status. Is he good to go in the three manly departments? And I'm not talking about manscaping. I'm talking about his house, his car, and his job. Then compare him to yourself and your status. If you're not on the same page, don't bother, it won't work. If your backgrounds are completely different, give it a shot but do not force the relationship. These are common everyday mistakes that women make that eventually result in them wasting years of their lives with the wrong man.

You CAN change your life! I recently reinvented myself. I had always felt somewhat lost, undervalued, not my best self. I was tired of feeling like that. I was tired of looking in from the outside and feeling that I was alone. I was tired of feeling like I could do better, but I was stuck. I knew I could do more, and I wasn't, and that was eating me alive. So, I got started on myself. I was a smoker for nearly 10 years, I quit cold turkey. I used to hate running, now I run 5Ks every other weekend. I always dreamt of starting my own company, but I was too scared to fail so I never tried. I now have my own company. Reinventing yourself is not impossible. It is hard, very hard. But if you have the will to change, it can be done. People say you can't change, that you are who you are. I don't think that's true, to an extent. I'm living proof that's not true. It's constant work. If you want to be different, it doesn't just happen. You have to wake up every day and make the decision that you will be different. The mind is a very powerful thing and I want to convince you that you're capable of change, too. The hardest part is just convincing yourself you can do it. It took me 10 years, possibly even longer.

Change your outlook, change your life. The minute you change your outlook is the second your life starts to change. If you think like you're blessed, act like you're blessed and talk like you're blessed, eventually you will be blessed and your prayers will be answered whether you believe in a higher power or not. If you think you're the biggest thing in the universe, chances are you need to work on yourself. If you feel like you've reached your maximum potential, chances are you've done great for yourself, but there's always work that needs to be done. I may have quit smoking and started running, but I still raise my voice in situations where I don't necessarily have to. Learning to change is a process. But you can't change unless you admit there's a problem, regardless of what it is. If you eat too much shit cake, you start to feel like shit. You start to talk shit. You start to look like shit. Because it's not all about outer beauty, who you are on the inside reflects what you look like on the outside. Nobody knows you better than yourself and your spouse. If your spouse is telling you something, it's because they see you for what you are and because they love you enough to actually tell you. For years my husband would tell me how I smell like cigarettes, how unattractive it is that I smoke, that I am jealous of any woman, that I'm always sad. There was a lot more truth to what he was telling me than I wanted to let on. I knew I could be doing better and I wasn't doing better. I would look at women jogging as we drove down to the mall and I would be jealous because they were doing something that I knew I could do but I wasn't putting my energy toward. I would see women at parties that we'd go to who would just be dancing all night not having to take cigarette breaks and it bothered me because I knew that I wanted to quit but hadn't. I would rather wallow in self-pity than do something about it. My husband called me for what I was, but I didn't do anything about it until I saw myself through his eyes.

Everyone blossoms in their own time. I've been with my husband for nine years. We finally just got married in January of 2021, after eight years of engagement and nine years together. People who don't know us may be confused as to why it took us so long; however, there was plenty we needed to change about ourselves before we could make that commitment. I completely changed my lifestyle, and Bond is working on changing his. The more that he sees me working on myself, trying to be better and do better, it motivates him. He's my soulmate, and sometimes we feed off each other's energy to survive. I definitely fed off of his for the first six years. He stood by me when I was at my lowest, when I was most confused, when I had lost all hope. He never gave up on me. He was always my light at the end of the tunnel. He always motivated me during those dark times. He was my lighthouse in the darkest of days and I am forever grateful. Now that I'm at a higher point in my life, I'm more than willing to share my energy, positivity, and aura with my man. That's what a relationship is about. Everyone blossoms in their own time. Flowers have different seasons to bloom for a reason. What's most important is that you're on the same page with your significant other or at least trying to be. It takes a lot of energy to make a relationship work, a lot of headaches a lot of heartaches, a lot of tears, a lot of sweat, a lot of bodily fluids, but nothing beats true love.

SUMMARY

Love is everywhere. What kind of love are you looking for? True love, best friend love, mother/son love, mother/daughter love, brotherly love, sisterly love? There are many types of love, and it all starts with you.

IN THE END

Not all men are the same. Not all women are the same. There is someone for everyone, and in knowing yourself, you will find the right person. Throughout this book, you've heard that you need to love yourself first. That's the damn truth. But you also need to know who you're looking for. What type of man is meant for you? If you don't know, or if all the different types sounded good, then darling, you still have some soul searching to do. Once a woman knows what she likes and dislikes, a whole new world opens up for her. An unimaginable, exciting new world.

Explore the world, yourself, your interests, and you'll learn what you do and don't like in a man. You'll be able to know a character from a mistake within seconds, and you can potentially save yourself years of headaches and heartaches. It's important to listen to that sixth sense we all have, and if you don't have it, tune into it. It's there, you just need to become one with yourself and the sense will reveal itself.

Since starting this book eight years ago, a close friend of mine got married and divorced. My sister was married and divorced. Another couple close to me separated, and another is still together. I started this book after I met my husband. And we've been married for one month now. My brother's been separated twice and is now back with his wife. My parents were separated and got back together. And my best friend Margarita found love, where Dee is still single and soul searching. All these situations are okay. They are normal.

My information collection on the different men and their personality types has been in progress for over 20 years. I've been collecting data, stories, interviews and personal experiences so I can share this with you today. I can tell you with confidence that some men will always stay the same personality type. However, there are men who will change. Just like you can change after soul searching. Men can do just the same. So, if you ever find yourself falling for a man who isn't The One, take your time. Keep finding yourself, learn what you love, and come back to it. Rome wasn't built in a day, and neither was the Hallmark channel. Love takes time, patience, and heartbreak. You'll need to stay strong through the experiences and trust your gut. Your inner voice is never wrong, and when you're up late crying or tossing and turning because you can't sleep, take a pen and paper, or open your notes app, and start jotting down how you're feeling. Why are you feeling this way? Who made you feel this way? What can be different? How can it be different? Who's in control to change the circumstance(s)?

We aren't stuck in life or in love. If something is off, or not working, then fix it, break it, or buy a new one. Whatever you need to be happy, that's what you need to do.

When you find someone who loves you truly, madly, deeply, they'll accept you for everything you are – flaws and all. They'll consider your flaws to be an asset, and they'll consider your good traits as what makes them love you. They will love you if you love yourself. A confident woman is a sexy woman.

I used to cry myself to sleep. I used to sleep around to find love. I used to do a lot of things that weren't me. The day I met Bond, I knew I had to better myself. I wish I'd had a book like this to help guide me through the darkest times. You're not alone. I wasn't alone. You have people who love you, whether you know it or not, and they'll be the best support system you could ever need.

If I was able to find true love, then anyone can find true love.

I thank The Character, The Sweetheart, The Bad Boy, The Mistake, and all the other men for making me who I am today. If it weren't for them, I wouldn't be Cindy. And if I wasn't Cindy, well then, who would I be?

ABOUT THE AUTHOR

Cindy lives in the Tampa Bay area with her amazing husband and two loud kids. Before she started writing her self-help book, Cindy almost got a bachelor's degree in Information Studies from the University of South Florida. After that, Cindy launched her career as a Marketing Manager for a cybersecurity company. Creativity, lateral thinking, attention to detail, along with focus and clarity are just some of the qualities Cindy contributes in her work. When she isn't working, you'll find Cindy chasing down her kids, reading on the beach, and running 5K's.

RICHTER
PUBLISHING

www.ingramcontent.com/pod-product-compliance
Lightning Source LLC
Chambersburg PA
CBHW071132090426
42736CB00012B/2100